C000162705

God's little people:

Little people
in Paul's letters

DayOne

© Day One Publications 2005
First printed 2005

ISBN 1 903087 85-6

9 781903 087855

Unless otherwise stated, all Scripture quotations are from the
New International Version copyright © 1973, 1978, 1984

British Library Cataloguing in Publication Data available

Published by Day One Publications
Ryelands Road, Leominster, HR6 8NZ
☎ 01568 613 740 FAX 01568 611 473
email—sales@dayone.co.uk
web site—www.dayone.co.uk
North American—e-mail—sales@dayonebookstore.com
North American—web site—www.dayonebookstore.com

Designed by Steve Devane and printed by Gutenberg Press, Malta

Contents

There is a long and honourable military tradition that an officer in the British armed services who is particularly commended for his courageous or exemplary action, will have his name recorded in the military annals. He may not gain the highest honours of service to his country, but his name is 'mentioned in dispatches', and he is henceforth entitled to wear a small bronze oak leaf on his right breast or on that campaign medal ribbon.

Someone has commented that 'the greater part of God's work in the world may go unnoticed.' This is true, because in the history of the Christian church our eyes are focused too often upon the big names that have come down to us: names of those who set the theological record straight, carved out new territories for the gospel, or held the line heroically in the face of overwhelming opposition. We have read their stories, and we are grateful for them. But as with any record of history, these tell only a part of the big picture. Everyone who knows anything about British history and our constant squabbles with the French, will know the name of Wellington—the 'Iron Duke'. But to say that Wellington beat the French at the battle of Waterloo is far from the truth: fifteen thousand Allied men died in the carnage of that savage battlefield, and most of them were ordinary infantrymen—but without them Wellington would have had no battle to fight and no victory to win. Yet how many historians could name even one common soldier who stood on the field of battle that fateful day on 18 June 1815?

The scene, sadly, is little different in our Christian history. By the end of the fourteenth century, John Wycliffe and his team had translated the Bible into English from the Latin Vulgate. For the first time, the Englishman could read the Bible in his own language. Thousands did, and what we can only describe as a spiritual revival must have swept across the country. The evidence of this is the fact that almost one hundred and twenty years later, Sir Thomas More, the ill fated Chancellor to Henry VIII, complained that you could not meet two men on the road of England without 'one of them being a Wycliffite'. But who knows the names of those thousands of ordinary labourers and artisans who maintained the light of the gospel at the hazard of their lives? Where is the earthly register of those who read, or listened to others read, the word of God for the first time in a language they understood, and then went out and told others what they had heard—who in turn passed it on to others until a whole nation was coming alive to the knowledge of God's word?

Without these 'little people' there would have been no tinder available to fuel the fire when William Tyndale gave England its first printed New Testament in 1526. And so the cycle repeated itself until the evangelical gospel became an unstoppable force in the land. And the chief work was done by those whose names are entirely unknown to us today. They carried Bibles, hidden under cart-loads of hay, across the mud-filled, rutted tracks of our countryside and then died in the stinking cellars of a bishop's palace for doing so. These were the common foot-soldiers of the gospel; unknown infantrymen of the cross. For every one whose name blazes across the pages of our heritage of history in the large letters of a Wycliffe, Tyndale, Latimer, Bunyan, Wesley, Whitefield, Spurgeon or Lloyd-Jones, there are tens of thousands of little people who have courageously and faithfully maintained a stand for the truth and have extended the borders of the Kingdom of God—and still do. It is upon these that the Lord builds his church, and the gates of hell will never prevail against it.

As if to set us an example in this, God has developed for us a theology of the little people. You will find this throughout the Bible. Little people are important in God's large strategy for the gospel, and the Bible is unique among the religious books of the world in its careful concern for individuals: A captive maid in Aram, a poor widow in Judea, a broken prostitute in Palestine, a business woman in Philippi, a kindly housemother in Joppa—these are just some of the many who flit across the pages of Scripture and who, but for the careful chronicling of the Holy Spirit, would have been lost to history for ever.

In particular, the letters of Paul have set us an example that is too often overlooked by those who leave us the records for historians to pore over. One fact among many that makes the New Testament such a thrilling book to read is the attention paid to these little people, and the value of this is that most of us are precisely that: little people. We will never be remembered much beyond our immediate generation, but we can all, nevertheless, leave a legacy that will reap its value as an investment for generations to come.

It is a tribute to the wise and understanding leadership of the greatest missionary evangelist of all time—the apostle Paul—that we have the stories in his letters of so many little people. A mark of small-minded and insecure leaders is their inability to commend others for fear of someone usurping their own supposed prestige or status. Commendation and appreciation are the calling cards of good leaders and are normally absent from the vocabulary of poor leaders. In Paul's great letter of Christian theology, he outlined for the church at Rome the history of redemption from creation to the end of time and introduced his readers to the momentous acts of God and the magnificent arrangement of salvation. At the close of his letter, this great theologian, evangelist, church planter, and ultimately martyr for the gospel of Christ, spent time sending personal greetings to nearly thirty Christians, eleven of whom are women. People mattered more than anything else to Paul. Ordinary people—little people. He refers to 'my dear friend Epenetus', 'Mary, who worked very hard for you', 'Andronicus and Junias, my relatives who have been in prison with me', 'Ampliatus, whom I love in the Lord', 'Urbanus, our fellow worker in Christ', 'my dear friend, Stachys', 'Apelles, tested and approved in Christ' , 'Tryphena and Tryphosa, those women who worked hard in the Lord' and a host more. And of each of these we know no more than Paul reveals in these brief phrases—but they were all people who mattered, and without whom there would have been no gospel and therefore no church for succeeding millennia.

This book will therefore be the story of some of the little people in whom Paul took great delight when he introduced them into his letters. God's theology of little people is a lesson of encouragement for *every* Christian faithfully at work in the church today.

In order to focus on the people, I have kept application to a minimum. This is not to suggest that applying the lessons of their lives is unimportant; on the contrary, Paul's encouragement that 'everything that was written in the past was written to teach us' (Romans 15:4), includes not only the Hebrew Scriptures but all parts of the New Testament also. However, my primary concern has been to bring these characters alive by understanding them in their cultural and historical setting and then to explain precisely what the writer's commendation means. The rest should be obvious. There are times when only the most spiritually blind will fail to learn the lessons from a life lived for the glory of God. I did not want constant application to get in the way of the real person. Their lives speak for themselves.

But all of these stories are incomplete. One of the great privileges of heaven—that place of perfect communication—will be the opportunity to meet with these same people, and millions more like them, and listen to the full story of their life and work. Then we shall know perfectly what the New Testament writers can only tell us in part. And the retelling of their stories, and our own, will be to the eternal honour of our triune God and Saviour.

Epaphroditus—an honourable soldier

'Honour men like him' Philippians 2:29

Whated Nero became Emperor of Rome in AD 54, at the age of seventeen, the future looked good. For a while the empire enjoyed sound and fair government—perhaps because one of Nero's advisers was the wise philosopher Seneca. Nero respected the Senate, curbed public violence and extortion, and even limited some of the worst excesses of the gladiatorial contests in the arena. But it was all short lived, and the behaviour and rule of this weak-eyed, pot-bellied, Emperor became increasingly bizarre, cruel and vicious. He murdered his mother and his wife, and ordered to commit suicide any senators, generals, and nobles whom he disliked — even his wise and loyal adviser, Seneca, was forced to take his own life.

In AD 64 a terrible fire in Rome destroyed a vast area of the city, and the speed with which Nero cleared the devastated area and began building his fabulous Golden Palace and its ornamental gardens, led to the suspicion that he had deliberately started the blaze. To turn attention away from himself, Nero blamed the new and increasing religion of Christians. They provided an easy distraction because they were already known as 'atheists', having abandoned the gods of the Roman pantheon. In the resulting persecution, hundreds of Christians were tortured, crucified, thrown to wild animals in the arena, or burnt to death to illuminate Nero's extravagant garden parties. But as the empire slipped into chaos, even this 'side show' could not hold the failing Emperor in power, and by January AD 68 his governors and generals were one by one withdrawing their oath of allegiance. Finally, Galba, an old veteran of many battles, let the Senate know that he was available if required, and the Senate roused itself, turned against the emperor, and ordered that Nero should be flogged to death. On 9 June AD 68, to pre-empt the Senate, Nero fled from Rome and committed suicide. In that final act he was assisted by his secretary—a freedman named Epaphroditus!

Four years earlier, in the same city and just before the great fire, Paul was under house arrest and he wrote a letter to the Christians at Philippi. That letter would be carried by one of the members of the church who had for some time been a companion of Paul in Rome. The name of that man was also Epaphroditus—but this one was a man to be honoured.

I have no doubt that Paul occasionally despaired of some of the Christian workers that he came into contact with. After working with him for so long, he discovered that Demas had all along been in love with the world; Phygelus and Hermogenes failed to support him when he most needed them; Hymenaeus and Philetus were spreading heresy like a gangrene; Alexander the Coppersmith caused Paul great harm; Alexander and Hymenaeus were in love with their own opinions, and Euodia and Syntyche were in love with their personal rights. At one time the apostle wrote sadly to Timothy: 'All have deserted me'; and he stood alone at his first defence before the Roman Emperor Nero. Writing to the Philippians here in 2:21 Paul must have despaired as he sadly penned: 'Everyone looks out for his own interests, not those of Jesus Christ.' Fortunately the 'everyone' was a general statement expressing Paul's bitter disappointment with so many Christians, because he immediately qualified it in the case of Timothy (v 22) and Epaphroditus (vs 25–30). Of Timothy Paul can confidently affirm, 'You know he has proved himself'. But so had Epaphroditus.

Paul's relationship with the church at Philippi, a proud and important city in the Roman province of Macedonia, began fourteen years earlier and is recorded in Acts 16. It is a most interesting story: Lydia was converted quietly down by the riverside; a slave girl was converted publicly and noisily and with the high drama of a riot that followed; and the city jailer was converted when his prison collapsed around him. Of all the towns Paul visited, Philippi was quite an experience even by the measure of Paul's exciting life. Although Luke does not tell us about him in his letter to Theophilus (Acts 1:1), one of the most exciting conversions at Philippi must have been that of a man called Epaphroditus. It was an exciting conversion if only because of the astonishing change in his life.

Encouragingly for Paul, the Christians at Philippi never wavered in their support of the apostle in his mission work, and even in their infancy they gave again and again to supply his needs. At one time they were the only church to provide regular encouragement in this way (4:14–16). Undoubtedly it was this very church that Paul had in mind when, in order to goad the Corinthians into action, he referred to the 'overflowing joy and rich generosity' of the Macedonians (2 Corinthians 8:1–5). Here was a church that literally 'pleaded' for the privilege of sharing in the service of giving to the needs of the poor Christians in Judea—but only after they had given 'themselves first to the Lord and then to us' (v 5). So Epaphroditus came from an outstanding Church: generous in giving to famine relief, consistent in their support of mission, and all with an enthusiasm and warm heart that was exemplary for the other churches to follow. Any man who represented such a church, and Epaphroditus did, had a high standard to reflect.

'My brother'

Like so many of these characters who flit briefly across the pages of the New Testament, we do not know much about Epaphroditus beyond what Paul mentions in the letter in front of us. He has a Greek name that is significant because it implies that as a baby his parents dedicated him to the goddess of love—Aphrodite. The Romans referred to her under the name Venus, the Syrians called her Astarte, and the Babylonians, Ishtar. She was well known. But this was certainly not a name that any Jewish parents would have given to their child. Doubtless his parents meant well because she was also the goddess of family life (though in some aspects the goddess of sex and lust also). Having been dedicated to a Greek goddess at the very moment of his birth, he was clearly brought up in a pagan environment. So when Paul referred to him in v 25 as 'my brother' we must appreciate the marvel of a gospel that can change people so radically. Here was Paul, a born and educated Jew, a rising star among the strictest Pharisees and an upcoming lawyer; one who all through his life tried to put the only true God first and was proud of his heritage and who hated idolatry and despised the life style of the pagans. He is now writing to a man who was brought up from birth as a pagan worshipper of the goddess of love and lust, and he calls him: 'my brother'.

Perhaps it is hard for us to understand the significance of that simple phrase 'my brother'. These two men would have had nothing in common with each other. Their religions put them worlds apart and each had no interest in the life style of the other. Certainly Saul of Tarsus would keep his distance; they had a totally different outlook upon life. But something had changed them both equally. When Christ came into their lives, all the barriers crashed into the sand. One of the great privileges of being a Christian is that here there is no colour, race, language, previous religion or no religion, that causes a barrier between the people of God. True Christianity brings together men and women of all abilities, interests, backgrounds, environments and approaches to life—they are all poured into the greater cause of serving the King of kings.

'My brother' was not just a statement that the apostle made because it seemed to be good for the unity of the Roman Empire, nor was it a statement he made because he believed that we should all pool our religious resources and assume that everyone has a little of the truth but that nobody has much—and certainly no one has all. In Christ these men had discovered the whole truth, and whilst the one looked back to his paganism and the other to his Judaism, both would say, 'I count them as rubbish for the sake of finding Christ'. That little phrase 'my brother', speaks volumes for the grace and mercy of God in bringing sinners like Paul and Epaphroditus into the family of God's people.

A trusted messenger

It is clear that Epaphroditus was more than a brother, he was a trusted messenger, because he had been sent with money from Philippi to Paul. The gifts that Epaphroditus brought with him were clearly of various kinds—because Paul used the plural 'gifts'—and, by the way Paul referred to them, they were generous gifts as well; this prisoner was 'amply supplied' by their 'fragrant offering', which was generously given and was acceptable to God (4:18).

Epaphroditus was in Rome as a messenger from the Philippian church to help Paul in his particular need at the present time. The money, and whatever else, was to support him in his imprisonment. A prisoner had to pay for his keep and he could literally starve if he had no money or no friends to bring him meals. But Paul was always more interested in people than in possessions, and he made this abundantly clear to the Christians at Corinth when he told them: 'What I want is not your possessions, but you' (2 Corinthians 12:14). The Philippians had modelled this for them (2 Corinthians 8:1–5). Helpful though the gift from Philippi was—and Paul thanks them for it profusely before he closes this letter—it was the man who came with it that Paul appreciated far more.

What God wants from every Christian first, is not that we dig deeper into our pockets but that we become the kind of people he wants us to be. It is not even talents, skills and gifts—however useful they are, or even the hard work we put in—and that too is vital. It is the quality of life that we live among the people of God and in the world around us that counts.

'Fellow-worker'

Paul would like to have kept Epaphroditus with him, but there were special reasons that dictated he should send him back to Philippi. What made this man so valuable to Paul and the gospel? Verse 25 tells us he was a 'fellow-worker'. It is not the first time that Paul used that phrase, and it will not be the last time that we meet it. Paul loved to have Epaphroditus around because he was an 'up and doing' man—and that certainly meant that he was a man in the pattern of Paul's own mind; certainly Paul set an example to the believers in all the churches for he could say to the Christians at Corinth: 'I worked harder than all of them.' Sadly, it has to be said about many Christians that it doesn't matter whether they are around or not; in fact, things often tick along more harmoniously if they are not around! But Epaphroditus was a worker. Becoming a Christian involves becoming a worker.

More than this, he was a *fellow*-worker. In the Greek it is the word 'worker' with a little prefix bolted on to the front that means 'with'. Paul wrote to the Corinthians and told them 'we are God's fellow-workers' (1 Corinthians 3:9). The *Authorised Version* translates it: 'labourers together with God'. That is good; it refers to those who are working hard *together*, and with God. The same word is used of Priscilla and Aquila—a wonderful husband and wife team who offered an open home wherever there was gospel work to do. And it is used also of Urbane, Timothy, Titus,

Clement, and Philemon. It is the word for a labourer, someone who is ready for anything and who considers nothing too small or too mundane to get on with. When Peter addressed leaders in the church, he reminded them of the servanthood of ministry and expected that all Christians, whether leaders or not, should work as humble servants of one another (1 Peter 5:1–6).

But you can be a worker without being a *fellow*-worker. When it comes to work in the church, the New Testament never thinks of professional classes and labouring classes. All are labourers. Equally, there is no place for the Christian who always wants to go it alone. Some Christians work hard but not in harmony; they always seems to be working against what the leaders or their fellow members are doing; perhaps they consider that they alone are right, or that they have a divine call to slow the work down; sometimes it is that their character is so abrasive that they can never work with others for long.

'Fellow-soldier'

Epaphroditus was valuable not only because he was a fellow-worker but because he was a fellow-soldier. These were dangerous days under the cruel rule of Nero. Some Christians are workers but they are not soldiers; they work well and hard but they forget that they are involved in a spiritual warfare. Paul wrote to the Ephesians about the armour of God and he reminded them that they were not fighting against flesh and blood but against spiritual forces; he encouraged Timothy to 'fight the good fight of the faith'. Peter warned his readers that they were fighting a battle against their own evil desires: the devil, wrote Peter, is our great enemy—and he knew that from bitter experience. Many Christians love this picture of warfare and soldiers: they glory in it and sing about it, but when the first shot is fired they are scuttling for cover.

Epaphroditus set us a good example. He was a man willing to risk his life for the cause of the gospel (v 30). At this point there are some small variations in the Greek texts available to us: some use the verb which means 'risk' or 'venture' or 'hazard', whilst others use a word referring to someone who is 'reckless' or 'regardless'. Either way it doesn't significantly change the meaning. I do not believe Epaphroditus was reckless in our modern sense, but he may have been regardless, just as Paul himself was: 'I consider my life worth nothing to me, if only I may finish the race and complete the task the Lord Jesus has given me—the task of testifying to the gospel of God's grace' (Acts 20:24). Here was a man who lacked a concern for himself; the one thing that mattered in Epaphroditus' life was not Epaphroditus, but that he might give himself unsparingly to the work of the gospel.

The Greek philosopher Aristotle was once caught looking into a shop window in Athens and someone chided him that he seemed to be going against all his philosophy by looking at the silver and gold items on show. His reply was: 'Oh I am not coveting them at all, I am just very grateful for the things I can easily do without.' Epaphroditus could do without many things for the sake of the gospel.

He risked his life—and the tense used here implies that it was a particular occasion. When and how, we are not told. Clearly he had been seriously ill and the same word is used in Luke 4:40 of 'various kinds of sickness'; but here Paul gives us no clue as to the nature of his illness. Saintly Murray McCheyne, who saw God work powerfully in his ministry in Scotland in 1839, once commented, 'A believer is to be known not only by his peace and joy, but by his warfare and distress.'

C.T. Studd, the missionary to Africa, referred to many Christians as 'Chocolate Soldiers': they melt away as soon as the heat is turned on. They love to sing the songs of warfare but they don't live as if they are in a warfare. The moment there is opposition, the call for personal sacrifice, the loss of popularity, or some kind of inconvenience, they are heard complaining that too much is demanded of them. Studd concluded, 'God was never a chocolate manufacturer and he never will be.'

Paul did not discuss whether or not Epaphroditus was wise in not taking care of his health, but he simply commended him for battling on in spite of it. We may think Paul was hard; in fact when we read Hebrews 12:4 we might even think that he was callous. There Paul reminded the Hebrew Christians that in their struggle against sin (persecution?) they had not yet resisted to the point of shedding their blood. That was supposed to be an encouragement! In other words he told them: 'Stop worrying about the problems you have in battling on in the Christian life, one thing you have not done yet is to shed your blood—that will come!' And in the next verse he continued: 'Do not make light of the Lord's discipline and do not lose heart when he rebukes you.' According to Paul, the Christian life is not meant to be easy. The easy part is waiting for us at the end, but now it is hard work and there is a battle to be fought.

There was a steady courage in this man Epaphroditus. Paul did not refer to anyone as a soldier unless he had well earned that tribute—and it *was* a tribute in Paul's mind. Whatever our views about the place of the Christian in earthly warfare, it is undeniable that it was a favourite picture of Paul, and this old soldier, who had been in the thick of many battles over the previous thirty years and bore the scars of many a close combat in his broken body, would never refer to a fellow Christian as a soldier unless that title was well deserved. Epaphroditus had certainly earned the title.

Soldiers are not trained in Bournemouth hotels but on Salisbury Plain. Captain Hugh McManners was a Commando in the brief Falklands War that began in April 1982. His task was to dig himself in on a hillside overlooking Port Stanley and disappear into his fox-hole during the day. At night he came out to direct naval gunfire over the town onto enemy positions. On the cold, wet hillside it was a miserable job. The ten thousand Argentine troops did not lack modern equipment, but most of the soldiers were conscripts and poorly trained. What turned the scales in this war that British soldiers fought eight thousand miles from home, was the rigorous training of the men; on 14th May the garrison at Port Stanley surrendered. In his book *Falklands Commando*, McManners concluded: 'It is the quality of the soldiers that counts, not the degrees of sophistication of equipment.' The church has never in its history had such sophisticated equipment available to it to communicate the gospel to the world, but—in the United Kingdom at least—rarely has it been so unsuccessful. What matters more than anything is the quality of its soldiers. We need an army of men like Epaphroditus.

But Epaphroditus was a *fellow*-soldier—it is that little prefix 'with' again. Imagine a battle where every soldier follows his own inclination; where each man fires in the direction he wants to fire, and in which each soldier is a law to himself and fights without regard for the man or platoon to his right and left and with no reference to the officer in charge? Queen Boudicca of the Iceni threw perhaps as many as two hundred thousand wild Celts at a mere fifteen thousand Roman legionaries drawn up somewhere north of St Albans in the year AD 60—and she lost! The total rout of her army was due solely to the incoherent charge of the Celts and the impeccable discipline of the Roman legions in their steady and relentless wedge formation as each man worked as bound to his neighbour. During the battles against the fierce Highlanders in Scotland in the eighteenth century, the English generals soon learnt an important lesson that they passed to their men: the infantry with their fixed bayonets were often outmanoeuvred by the fast slash of a sharp double-edged sword to their right side; so the order went out for each infantryman to lunge his bayonet at the enemy approaching to his left, 'and leave the man to your right to take care of the enemy to your right'. That took some trust in your colleague to the right! But when every man worked *with* his neighbour, the battle could be won.

The British army is acknowledged as producing arguably the best soldiers in the world for their discipline in battle and its aftermath, but they are also exceptionally good in the art of parade and display. Tourists crowd to see the colourful Trooping of the Colour and the guards outside Buckingham Palace and elsewhere in the capital. The precision and attention to detail when a whole regiment moves as one man is an awesome sight. But is there no connection between the fighting ability of those men and their marching and wheeling in full regalia and with awesome precision to the admiration of gawping tourists? Of course there is. They were learning to work together so that they could fight together; that is the secret of their success. It is precisely because so many in the church cannot work together that they cannot fight the real enemy effectively either. Paul valued highly Christians like Epaphroditus who worked *with* his comrades in the cause of the gospel, rather than squabbling over 'foolish and stupid arguments' that produce quarrels (2 Timothy 2:23).

Caring companion

Epaphroditus was not only a courageous and well disciplined soldier, he was also a caring companion. He was sent to 'take care' of Paul (v 25); although the word used here (*leitourgos*) can have a reference to military service, and often also refers to religious service in the temple (it is used of

Christ in Hebrews 8:2, even the angels in Hebrews 1:7, and Paul used it of himself in Romans 15:16). Its more general use is with reference to someone who is appointed to serve in public office at their own expense. But it is the appointment that is important. They do not serve just on their own account. Epaphroditus had been sent by the church at Philippi, perhaps at his own expense, to take care of Paul's needs.

The whole church at Philippi could hardly uproot, walk to Rome and settle down with Paul in his house arrest (v 30), but they wanted to send a man who would act as their 'messenger' (v 25). The word used here is the word for 'apostle', which literally means 'one who is sent'; it is used in a non-technical sense and we can take it to refer to Epaphroditus as their 'messenger boy'. But they were looking for one who would represent the heartbeat of the whole church and in that sense would carry the true message of the church with him. Epaphroditus was the man who would best express the relationship that the church at Philippi had with Paul. If your church had to choose one Christian from the congregation to send to Paul in Rome—someone who could be trusted with a sizeable gift for the apostle and who would bring encouragement and care to him as well—whose name would head the list?

But the heart of Epaphroditus is also seen in his response when he heard that the church back in Philippi was anxious over his recent illness. He had been seriously ill—near to death—and he heard that the church in Philippi was distressed for him, and he in turn became anxious about their anxiety! A strong word is used here and 'distraught' would be a good translation; this precise word is used of the agony of Christ in Gethsemane when he was 'sorrowful and troubled' (Matthew 26:37)—over his disciples? I wonder if Paul became more concerned for Epaphroditus' state of anxiety than he was over the original illness. How ill he had been can be seen by Paul's reference to the fact that he almost died and that when he recovered it was to spare Paul 'sorrow upon sorrow'—the word 'sorrow' was commonly used for mourning.

Some time ago in our church it was announced at a prayer meeting that a certain member might have to move away because of their work. One member commented in prayer that if that particular member left, 'it would be like a funeral for us.' That is exactly how Paul felt about the departure of

Epaphroditus for Philippi. The only encouragement was that he hadn't died—that would have been 'sorrow upon sorrow'. Because of his anxious care for his friends back home, Epaphroditus longed to be with them again; the strength of this is seen in the fact that Paul himself used the same word to express his own love for the church there: 'I long for all of you with the affection of Christ Jesus' (1:8). When Christians in the local church feel this way about one another, then there is such a relationship that will be a magnetic attraction to the harsh world outside.

Interestingly, Paul says very little about this man's recovery. Perhaps it was a miraculous recovery in answer to prayer—certainly Paul would have been praying for him—or perhaps they rubbed in some oil somewhere, or he swallowed some herbal remedy recommended by Dr Luke. Today that would be the big thing to report! But in his letters, Paul passes over miracles, signs and revelations with barely a mention. Today what are considered awesome among Christians are things like prophecies, miracles, wonders, and phenomena. But for Paul, what was awesome was the quality of a man so tough that he carried on his Christian life like the bravest and most unselfish of soldiers and yet so tender that his heart and mind were desperately anxious even to know that other Christians were worried about him. That man was Epaphroditus.

What is amazing is a man or a woman who can live out the fruit of the Spirit in a pagan world every day, or a Christian who, in spite of all circumstances, keeps on and encourages others to do the same. What is awesome is the Christian mother of four lively youngsters who at the end of the day is still sweet tempered and calm and who creates a home of peace, or the Christian businessman who after a day of frustration in the office, is loving to his wife and children when he walks through the front door. What is remarkable is the Christian worker who doesn't make an issue when put out by other people's thoughtlessness. Give us men and women like this in the church and you can keep most other signs and wonders.

Welcome him

This man who had been dedicated from birth to the goddess of love—with all the pagan trappings that went along with it—was transformed to become a brother in Christ, a Christian worker, fellow-soldier and a caring companion. Little surprise, therefore, that Paul encouraged the Philippian church to make sure that there would be a very special home-coming for this faithful warrior. First they are to 'welcome' him. You will find the word used of our Lord's reception of sinners in Luke 15:2, and Paul encouraged the church at Rome to 'receive' Phoebe in the same way (Romans 16:2). And this is to be done with 'great joy'.

Then they are to 'honour' him. The significance of this word is that it was sometimes used in the first century to refer to a soldier's 'honourable discharge'. That would be a familiar expression to the folk in Philippi because there was a veritable 'Dad's Army' in residence in the city and its surrounding villages with many Roman veterans settled in the area; a pension and a plot of land was their reward for twenty years service in the legions of the Emperor. Perhaps some of these old soldiers were in the congregation. I doubt whether a man like Epaphroditus would ever consider himself discharged from Christian service, but he was certainly to be received by his fellow believers just as a well-decorated legionary would be honoured. The same word also refers to the preciousness of Christ to his Father in 1 Peter 2:4; as the Father places a high value upon his Son, so the church should place a high value upon men and women like Epaphroditus.

The church can live and grow without spectacular gifts, miraculous signs, titillating phenomena and fantastic revelations—but it will shrivel and die without men and women like Epaphroditus.

John Mark—God's remould

'Get Mark and bring him with you, because he is helpful to me in my ministry.' 2 Timothy 4:11

When it comes to replacing the tyres on my car I have always been very suspicious of remoulds, or retreads as they are sometimes known. They seem to me to be untrustworthy by definition and I would always be thinking not about what they are but what they were. But that is exactly what a Christian is—a remould. The sovereign Creator takes us—spoiled and worn by sin, rebellious and utterly unfit for his service—and like a perfect and wise potter he remoulds us to make us pleasing to himself. And the mould to which we are fashioned is the perfect pattern of his Son Jesus Christ. All through our Christian life we are still being worn and damaged by sin and God takes us as often as we need and he remoulds us; each time the remould is a little closer to the great pattern that he intends for me: 'So the potter formed it into another pot, shaping it as seemed best to him' (Jeremiah 18:4).

The Christian mentioned by Paul in 2 Timothy 4:11 was a perfect example of one of God's remoulds. He was such a significant first-term failure that he caused a major rift between two senior colleagues that threatened the unity of the early gospel work. But God so remoulded John Mark that the last mention of him in the New Testament is one of the most positive that anyone could hope for—and the only mention he receives outside the Bible is even better! But first we must look at his life before Paul made reference to him.

The spoilt son of a wealthy widow?
John Mark has two names: *John* is his Jewish name which is short for 'Jonathan' and appropriately means 'the Lord has shown grace'. His other name is *Marcus* which is clearly an adopted name and, since it is Roman, may add to the suggestion that he came from a family of rank and influence, property and wealth. Presumably the two names are used in

order to distinguish him from the apostle John. Clearly he was brought up in Jerusalem and his mother was one of the six Marys mentioned in the New Testament. It is suggested that the Last Supper was held in his house and the owner of the house referred to in Mark 14:14 was therefore his father; this is likely though not certain.

What is certain is that John Mark's house became a regular meeting place for the early Christians in Jerusalem, because when Peter was angelically released from prison, he immediately knew where to find the rest of the disciples, and went straight to John Mark's home: 'Where many people had gathered and were praying.' If that was the same house the Christians were meeting in when the Holy Spirit came down at Pentecost, which is very likely, then the room was capable of seating around one hundred and twenty people at least. John Mark therefore came from a family of wealth, though possibly his father died early in his son's life.

According to Paul in Colossians 4:10, Barnabas, the son of encouragement whom we meet in Acts 4:36–37, was a cousin of John Mark. Barnabas was a Jew from Cyprus. Although we cannot be certain, it is quite possible that the young man referred to in Mark 14:51, who fled from Gethsemane at the time of Jesus' arrest, is John Mark himself; if so, that would put him in his teens around the time of the crucifixion and therefore in his early thirties when we meet him first by name in Acts 12:12.

John Mark clearly became a Christian worker and therefore he is a great encouragement for all who have at some point failed in their Christian life and service—which must surely be all! We have all failed in service, fallen in our Christian life, let others down, turned our back upon the work and opportunities for witness, and disappointed those who trusted in us. The fall and rise of this remarkable remould is instructive for all involved in Christian service.

John Mark came from a home with a strong Christian influence, at least his mother was a true follower of Jesus. The silence concerning his father may imply that his father had died by the time we meet John Mark, but his mother was clearly very hospitable. She had a big home and a Christian heart and she opened both. People came in and out of the home often, and prayer meetings—big ones and sometimes long ones—were a regular pattern of family life. It was a home that breathed the atmosphere of Christian conduct and service. That was a great privilege for John Mark.

But it was also a home of wealth and influence. John Mark was used to servants and therefore to comfort. And that was perhaps the start of his problems. Life was very comfortable; more comfortable for him than for many of his friends. There were things he did not have to do because there were servants in the home. Someone has referred to him as the 'spoilt son of a wealthy widow'. Perhaps he was overprotected; he never quite faced the real world. That he had a faith is certain, but it was a quiet and unassuming faith and it had not yet been tested; it had all been too easygoing for him. So, although his great strength was his Christian home, in that very privilege lay his inherent weakness. He relied upon his mother, perhaps his father also, and the security of the home. His faith had never been tested. Privileges like his always carry a potential for failure.

A missionary menace

Acts 12:25 informs us that when Paul and Barnabas returned from Jerusalem they brought with them to Antioch 'John, also called Mark'. There is little doubt that the young man was full of an enthusiasm which impressed those two Christian warriors. They were not fools and were generally good judges of people, so they invited John Mark to join them when they returned from Jerusalem to Antioch with great hopes for the future. He was serious and spiritual and came from a good Christian home. Barnabas may have been swayed by the family connection, but we can imagine John Mark when he arrived in Antioch in the company of Paul and Barnabas. The Christians were already beginning to see these two men as significant leaders in fulfilling the great commission. John came along with them, doubtless basking in the honour of being seen in such well respected company.

More than this. When the Holy Spirit told the church at Antioch to set aside Paul and Barnabas for the work of the gospel—and for pioneer evangelism at that—they chose John Mark as their helper. So far so good. He had clearly convinced them that he was the right man. The word used in Acts 13:5 describes him as a 'junior helper'; it originally referred to an 'under-rower' and was used of an assistant who busied himself in the service of a superior. It is not difficult to see what it meant for John Mark: when the church got down to prayer and sent off the mission team, he was on that team; when they got onto the boat and all the Christians were waving goodbye, he was on that boat—and he was enjoying every minute of it. But all of that compounded the future failure.

John Mark had never yet had to stand on his own, and the honour of his close association with Paul and Barnabas did not help him. Reflected glory is never authentically personal. Perhaps this lay behind Paul's advice to Timothy: The elder 'must not be a new convert, or he may become conceited and fall under the same judgement as the devil' (1 Timothy 3:6). And perhaps Paul also had John Mark in mind when he instructed Timothy: 'Do not be hasty in the laying on of hands' (1 Timothy 5:22); meaning, don't be too quick in setting people apart for the work of God—check them out thoroughly.

The first stop on the mission trail was Cyprus, which happened to be the home of Barnabas; and because Barnabas and John Mark were cousins, there were obviously a lot of relatives in Cyprus whom John Mark had not seen for a while—if ever—and as they travelled through the whole island there was plenty of time to meet up with them. He arrived among his relatives in company with Paul and Barnabas—no less! At Paphos, Elymas the sorcerer was beaten in spiritual combat with Paul, and the young recruit must have found that scary, although the outcome was a convincing victory for Christ (Acts 13:6–11), and John Mark could bask in the reflection of the spiritual power exercised by Paul. Then, to cap it all, the Proconsul of the island believed the gospel (v 12). John Mark perhaps thought that if things went on like this the whole empire would soon be Christian! If evangelism were as simple as this, he certainly wanted to be in on it. It was all very exciting—and just as he had anticipated when he set out with Paul and Barnabas. John Mark was a willing, enthusiastic and busy 'helper'.

Then one morning the missionary company boarded a ship and left Cyprus. When they next reached land John Mark found he had doubled the distance from home and was now five hundred miles (800 km) away from security. Perhaps for the first time in his life he was in territory with no known relatives and no Christian influence.

A mission leader gave me the top three reasons why some missionaries failed to make it through the first term. Here they are:

- Failure to keep close to God when you can't rely on your friends.
- Failure to handle cross-cultural relationships.
- The failure of the task to meet the expectations of the missionary.

John Mark hit all of these three. His Christian life had been relying not wholly upon Christ but upon his Christian friends and his family; life had been full of Christians, prayer meetings, Christian conversation, and the optimism of gospel success that followed Pentecost. At Perga in Pamphylia suddenly he was confronted with what he had never met before, not even on Cyprus.

Perga, now a ruin, was then the cultural and religious centre of the province of Pamphylia. Seven miles inland from its port at Attalia, it could boast a theatre, stadium and magnificently colonnaded and impressively wide streets. Above all, worship centred on the temple dedicated to Artemis (Diana to the Romans), and though the building was not so impressive or important as the one at Ephesus, she was nevertheless adored as 'The Queen of Perga'. This was a thoroughly pagan city situated on a lucrative trade route and therefore it was cosmopolitan. People from all over the world arrived here, and this meant there were languages and customs, food, smells and sights that John Mark had never before experienced. And there were few Jews and fewer Christians—if any. It clearly was not going to be easy in Perga. But there was something else very significant that may help to explain why John Mark deserted at this point so early in the campaign.

Perga was in the Roman province of Pamphylia, and although there may possibly have been a few Christians here as a result of Pentecost (Acts 2:10), no evangelism is recorded on this outward bound mission in either Perga itself or in the wider region of Pamphylia (Acts 13:13). In fact, in the following verse we find Paul and Barnabas in Pisidian Antioch which is one hundred miles (160 km) to the north. Why? Pisidian Antioch was on the borders of the territory known as Galatia, and when Paul later wrote to the churches in Galatia, he reminded them that he had first preached among them 'because of an illness' (Galatians 4:13). That illness was clearly severe (in v 14 Paul describes it as 'a trial to you'), but they lovingly cared for this wounded soldier. Whatever the illness—perhaps it was his recurring eye problem—this appears to have been the reason why Paul and Barnabas moved quickly from the coastal plain to the healthier higher ground of Antioch, three and a half thousand feet (over 1000 m) above sea level.

So, did Paul become seriously ill in Perga and decide to press on to the better climate in Pisidian Antioch where he knew that a large Jewish community lived? If so, this sudden change of plan in Perga, the lack of evangelistic success—or even endeavour, no sorcerers defeated, no city officials converted—the serious illness of the team leader, the alien culture all around him, and the imminent departure inland, was all too much for John Mark. The work was not living up to his expectations. Perhaps at this point he lost confidence in the whole campaign. The only fact of any significance recorded in this city is that 'John left them to return to Jerusalem' (Acts 13:13).

Often in Christian work the best and most carefully laid plans do not work out; this does not necessarily mean that something has gone wrong or that God has abandoned us, or that we have missed his plan. If John had 'hung on in there', he would have learned sooner a vital lesson that he would doubtless have to learn later: God moves in mysterious—and often to us unacceptable—ways. Learning that the will of God is 'good, pleasing and perfect' (Romans 12:2), is one of the hardest lessons in the Christian life. Paul himself was soon to become familiar with unexpected changes of plans: in Phrygia and Galatia (Acts 16:6), at Mysia (v 7), and in his longing to visit the Thessalonians which was frustrated by Satan (1 Thessalonians 2:18). Later, Paul also planned to travel from Corinth to Jerusalem and then call by at Rome on his way to Spain (Romans 15:24–25)—in the event it is doubtful that he ever reached Spain, having been arrested in Jerusalem and shipped to Rome as a prisoner where all his missionary vision abruptly ended in execution!

The words used in Acts 13:13 literally mean that John Mark 'turned back'. He must have made a stopover at Cyprus; but what kind of reason did he give for passing through quickly as he hurried back to Jerusalem? I imagine him suggesting that the organization of this mission work was a shambles—you can never be sure what will happen next. He had to learn that this is precisely the nature of front line gospel work! We can all find excuses for turning our back upon the work and avoiding the call of God. But within us we know what we are doing.

A missionary mistrusted

Almost three years later Paul and Barnabas had finished their first evangelistic tour and had returned to Antioch in Syria to report to the church there. Shortly after, they were sent to Jerusalem as delegates to the first ever conference of the fellowship of independent evangelical churches (Acts 15). Here they must have met with John Mark, and he was sufficiently confident in himself to accompany Paul and Barnabas back to Antioch. We pick up the story in Acts 15:36–40, 'Sometime later Paul said to Barnabas, "Let us go back and visit the brothers in all the towns where we preached the word of the Lord and see how they are doing." Barnabas wanted to take John, also called Mark, with them, but Paul did not think it wise to take him because he had deserted them in Pamphylia and had not continued with them in the work. They had such a sharp disagreement that they parted company. Barnabas took Mark and sailed to Cyprus, but Paul chose Silas and left, commended by the brothers to the grace of God.'

It is not surprising that those who let down others in a vital situation will not easily be trusted in the future. The damage potential of the failure of John Mark was enormous. We may wonder whether Paul and Barnabas had spent the previous three years working together with an uneasy agreement not to mention John's name! Family ties bred strong unity in that culture, and as they moved on to Pamphylia, Barnabas must have been embarrassed by the failure of his younger cousin. Paul, who perhaps exploded at the desertion, decided to let the matter drop and he may secretly have expected—and hoped?—that John Mark was consigned to history. But here he is again, and what is worse, all the old sores are reopened. Barnabas—ever with his generous spirit of encouragement—was all for taking John and giving him a second chance. Perhaps, beyond the family ties, Barnabas had an eye on the remould and could see potential in this failure.

This led to a 'sharp disagreement'. Significantly, the word is strong and originally referred to an 'irritation'. We can imagine Barnabas arguing the case and reminding Paul that *he* had once needed a loyal friend who trusted him when all others refused to (Acts 9:26–27), so perhaps Paul should trust Barnabas' judgment now—after all, Barnabas had not made a mistake on *that* occasion had he? Doubtless he drew attention to all the strong points in John's favour: his good background, youthful zeal, helpful nature, his readiness to come to Antioch being a sign that he had learnt his lesson, and so on.

Paul, on the other hand, saw John Mark's desertion as very serious. John had 'deserted' once before (that is an accurate translation because the word means 'stand apart' or 'shun'), and he was not prepared to take the risk again. In the application of the parable of the seeds scattered on the land, Jesus described the seeds that fell onto the rocks as those who are zealous for a moment and then in the time of testing they 'fall away'—they desert (Luke 8:13). That is the word Paul used here to describe John Mark. And in 1 Timothy 4:1, perhaps with John Mark in the back of his mind, the apostle Paul wrote that 'some will abandon the faith', that is the same word. For Paul, it was just too great a risk to take John Mark on this second evangelistic tour.

John Mark's desertion discouraged and divided the other Christians. Loyalty and dogged discipline are so encouraging, but to abandon the cause and give up the fight, simply discourages the rest of the workers. We can hardly blame either Paul or Barnabas. Both men had very good reasons for arguing as they did. Paul's standards demanded the highest quality of soldiers for the mission field. Barnabas, on the other hand, had an eye on the potential value of this failure. The tragedy lay in the serious clash between the two workers, but the triumph lay in their wisdom to agree to part. God frequently overrules our muddle and confusion for the welfare of his Kingdom. In the event a mission party did set out, and a training school was established as well.

The year was AD 49, and Barnabas took John Mark in hand and they headed for Cyprus—away from home but among relatives—and for the next twelve years or so we hear nothing more about either of them. That does not mean that nothing happened. When next we meet with John Mark he is not five hundred miles but fifteen hundred miles from home! Exactly what he is doing and where he is we will see in a moment.

Better the mistakes of the trainee than those of the Christian trusted with significant responsibilities. The better the training, the better the service. John Mark needed training, and if Paul and Barnabas had been less hasty in taking an untested recruit with them, he might have been ready for front line work sooner. Peter learned this. Jesus said to him: 'Peter Satan has desired to have you to sift you like wheat but I have prayed for you so that your faith will not fail, and when you have turned back, strengthen your brothers' (Luke 22:31–32). Notice the progression: 'Satan has … but I have … and when you have.' Satan appears to have it all his own way, but Christ has a better plan and when he has restored us we have a new future. That is what remoulds are all about.

A missionary matured

Around the year AD 63 Paul was a prisoner in Rome and had written a letter to the church at Colosse, a city in the Roman province of Asia a thousand miles east of Rome and five hundred and sixty miles west of Jerusalem. Two men were with Paul as he came to the close of this letter: one was called Aristarchus, and he asked Paul to be sure to send his greetings to the Christians at Colosse, though he was not free to travel because he was a prisoner along with Paul.

The other companion was John Mark—reunited with his old leader whom he had deserted twelve years earlier—and he was now clearly ready to visit Colosse. This is how Paul introduced the two men: 'My fellow-prisoner Aristarchus sends you his greetings, as does Mark, the cousin of Barnabas. You have received instructions about him; if he comes to you, welcome him' (Colossians 4:10). The way Paul wrote is significant. Word of the rift all those years earlier had got around and some would be surprised to find Paul and the first-term failure in the same company, so Paul made it clear just who he is referring to: 'You know which Mark I mean—the cousin of Barnabas'. And then Paul added significantly: 'You have received instructions about him; if he comes to you, welcome him'. What were those instructions? We are not told, but my guess is that it went like this: 'Listen, I know Mark deserted us some years back, but he is a different man now. Forget his past, and when he comes, welcome him. You'll be glad you did.'

But notice what else Paul said about him here in Colossians 4:11. John Mark is coupled with a man called Justus and together these men are described as the only Jews among Paul's fellow-workers. Interestingly, in Philemon—the letter that was sent along with this one to the Colossians— Paul used exactly the same title to refer to Mark: 'a fellow-worker' (v 24). A dozen years earlier John Mark had started out as a junior helper (Acts 13:5) and Paul soon had reason to complain that he was a deserter, but now the apostle commends him as a 'fellow-worker'. More than that, he and Justus are a 'comfort' to Paul: 'a soothing' is the word used; the verbal form refers to medicine that soothes an irritation. Once, John Mark was the biggest irritant around, but now he is the very thing that soothes irritation. Once Paul did not want him around, but now he cannot do without him. A failure in Pamphylia but a success in the cells of Rome. If Barnabas was wise enough to train him, Paul was big enough to give him another chance: 'I will repay you for the years the locusts have eaten' (Joel 2:25). But there was better to come.

A year or so later Paul was approaching the close of his life. Writing to Timothy at Ephesus he urged, 'Get Mark and bring him with you, because he is helpful to me in my ministry' (2 Timothy 4:11). So, if John Mark is not now with Paul, where is he? He must be on that mission to Colosse that the apostle wrote about to the Colossians, because the verb that Paul used implies that Timothy would need to fetch John Mark before he set out for Rome. Some three days journey from Ephesus, Colosse was another city straddling a trade route, and it was therefore a cosmopolitan population with many religions and cultures; a variety of languages were spoken in the market-place—not unlike Perga in Pamphylia of painful memory!

Whether Timothy and John Mark arrived in time we do not know, but we do know that he would have been 'helpful' to Paul, and the word used means 'easy to make use of'. That means that after nearly twenty years he was back to being the helper he wanted to be all along.

There is one more Bible reference to John Mark: this time he is with Peter in Rome, probably shortly after he and Timothy arrived there—perhaps too late to join Paul before his execution. Peter wrote, 'She who is in Babylon', which is probably a cryptic reference to the church in Rome, 'chosen together with you, sends you her greetings and so does my son Mark' (1 Peter 5:13). But now what is occupying John Mark's time? To answer this intriguing question we will listen in to part of a letter written by an early Christian leader called Papias around the year AD140: 'Mark, who was the interpreter of Peter, wrote down accurately all that he remembered, whether sayings or doings, of Christ; but not in order, for he was neither a hearer nor companion of the Lord. Mark made no mistakes when he wrote down thus all things as he remembered them, for he concentrated on this alone not to omit anything that he had heard nor to include any false statement among them.

In saying that Mark was not a 'hearer or companion of our Lord', Papias simply meant that Mark was not a regular disciple of Christ, because, living in Jerusalem, he clearly must have heard Jesus; and we have already suggested that he was the young man in Gethsemane referred to in Mark 14:51. Here then is the same John Mark who failed so miserably at Perga, now recounting all that he had heard from the mouth of the ageing Peter so that a new record of the life of Christ can be given to the churches. What is more to the point, this early disaster on the mission field is now entrusted by the Holy Spirit to be the channel for Scripture: 'Men spoke from God as they were carried along by the Holy Spirit' (2 Peter 1:21). You will find the result of that work in the *Gospel of Mark*.

The value of remoulds
From a first term failure abandoning the cause, deserting the colours and dividing the workers, John Mark became a valuable worker for the gospel, a vital friend of Paul—the very man he deserted—who now trusted him. He was now a fellow worker in the hard parts of the Empire, and the writer of our second Gospel which many believe was the very first one to have been written. Some remould! Is anything too hard for the Lord? If he did that with John Mark, is there anything he cannot do with any of us? My view of remoulds was changed when I read an article assuring me that remoulds were every bit as reliable and safe as a brand new tyre. There is always plenty of mileage left when we return to the God of remoulds.

Tychicus—a trusted messenger

'Tychicus will tell you all the news about me. He is a dear brother, a faithful minister and fellow-servant in the Lord' Colossians 4:7

Those little people who are mentioned in despatches are very easily overlooked in the New Testament records, and the reason for this is that our eyes are upon the prominent names. We are focussed on the ones who appear to be at the forefront of the combat, who harass the enemy in a big way—who storm the front line and gain significant battle honours. In Acts 20:4 we are presented with a list of men, some of whom pass swiftly across the field of conflict in the New Testament, but all of whom were quite clearly significant men in their own local churches.

Paul had been in Ephesus for two years, from AD 55–57 (Acts 19). From there he wrote a letter to the church at Corinth, informing them that on his way through to Jerusalem he would call by in order, among other things, to collect their gifts which they had set aside for the poor Christians in Judea. In 1 Corinthians 16:2–4 Paul laid out his instructions about putting the money aside each week and appointing trusted men who would accompany him with the Corinthian gift. The safe return of those men would be the receipt that the gift had arrived safely in Jerusalem and had been distributed among those in need.

On his way to Jerusalem Paul gathered the representatives of the churches, and by the time he arrived in Judea there would have been quite an assembly to check out the distribution of the money. The apostle provides us with a list of a few of the men involved. There were the Macedonians whom Paul held up to the Corinthians as a model of sacrificial giving (2 Corinthians 8:1–5): Sopater of Berea, and Aristarchus and Secundus of Thessalonica; then there was Gaius from Derbe in Pamphylia, and Timothy who was born in Lystra—though we are not told whether he was a delegate. Finally there are two men from Asia: Tychicus and Trophimus. Trophimus had no idea of the trouble he would cause—though by no fault of his own—when he arrived in Jerusalem with Paul;

through a misunderstanding by the Jewish mob, Paul was almost lynched and Trophimus himself was fortunate to escape with his life (Acts 21:27 on). The last we read of this unfortunate brother is in 2 Timothy 4:20 where Paul had left him ill at Miletus in the hope of recovery—whether he did recover or not history does not record. But Trophimus is not in focus for us here, because among that list is our man called Tychicus.

Tested and approved

Tychicus was a native of Asia, very likely from Ephesus itself. His name means 'fortunate', and since he had no settled ministry he was certainly fortunate in avoiding many of the problems that faced men like Timothy and Titus in their pastoral responsibilities at Ephesus and Crete. However, he was not a man to avoid dangerous situations and hard issues. Perhaps he was converted during Paul's second missionary journey across north Asia, but whilst he was very likely from a pagan background and certainly from a non-Jewish home, we know nothing more about his parents and upbringing. He must have been part of an inner circle of travelling friends, since Paul indicated that he was sending Tychicus to them because he knew exactly what was going on in Rome and would be able to tell them everything. He was, therefore, a close companion of Paul. One thing is absolutely certain: Tychicus was a man who could be relied on.

What Paul wrote to the church at Corinth during his two year stay at Ephesus, we may assume was true of all the churches when they elected special men to take their gift up to Jerusalem. They were to be men who are 'approved'. That word means to test or examine something before endorsement. When you take something off the shelf, examine it closely, and finally decide that it is fit for your use, that is the word used here. When Paul sent Titus to Corinth, he described an unnamed worker who accompanied Titus as one who in many ways 'has often *proved* to us that he is zealous' (2 Corinthians 8:22)—that is the same word; this unnamed messenger was known, examined, and approved by the Christians.

Before these men set out from their churches to accompany Paul to Jerusalem they had to be tested in their local congregation. Paul was absolutely clear about that. He would not send just anybody, anywhere; he would send only those who had been proved and finally approved, by their local church. This is one reason why the New Testament lays such stress upon the importance of the local church. Who else can validate our Christian service or, more importantly, our Christian life?

Not infrequently I am asked to comment upon ministers by way of a reference, and I am asked what I know about their pastoral work, their preaching and even their personal devotional life. The problem is that I cannot effectively comment upon these areas of a man's life unless I have sat under his preaching for some time and unless I have experienced his pastoral care, or lived in his home for a while. But I can tell you who will know: the people among whom he has been preaching and among whom he has carried out his pastoral responsibilities for some years. His local church can tell you something about him. That is how and why these were the men chosen. They did not merely give a good impression—that is quite easy to do—but the people among whom they lived and worked knew what they were really like.

Tychicus was a man of total honesty, he had been proved and tested and therefore he carried the money up to Jerusalem on behalf of the churches in Asia. There ought to be a plain straightforward honesty and integrity about Christians that is remarkable in this dishonest world. Every Christian should be tried and tested by their local church and proved to be honest and upright in every way; it is not sufficient to assume integrity simply because a man belongs to the people of God. This was one of the most important things about Tychicus, because it was the foundation without which nothing reliable could be built. Nothing else would be true of him; if he failed there he would have failed everywhere. At Ephesus there were two men who stood out as men of integrity: Tychicus and Trophimus; they were utterly reliable. There were doubtless others, but these men were outstanding and available.

However, even more significant than the fact that Tychicus was entrusted with cash, was the fact that Tychicus was entrusted with a very important letter. In AD 62 Paul found himself a prisoner at Rome, and among the letters he wrote from his house arrest was the one addressed to the Ephesians. From Ephesians 6:21–22 it is clear that Tychicus was the messenger who carried that letter to the church at Ephesus.

There are a few old Greek manuscripts of this letter that omit the words 'in Ephesus' in the first verse, and this has given rise to the suggestion that the letter to the Ephesians was originally a circular letter that Tychicus carried around with him—a whole bundle of copies—and he simply filled in the name of the church in Asia that he happened to be visiting. In other words, he took this round robin, delivered it personally and wrote in the name as he came to the church. That may be a nice theory, but it is not very convincing since most Greek texts, all the versions (the translations of the Greek texts in the first three centuries), and all the early church leaders of those centuries, knew that this was a letter addressed to the church at Ephesus. The fact that the name is missing from a few Greek texts simply means that it was later copied and passed round other churches. But originally it was sent to the church at Ephesus. There can be no serious doubt about that.

However what is more important as far as we are concerned is that Tychicus was given a position of great trust to carry this letter and not to meddle with it. Already there were those—Paul refers to them in his letters as 'false apostles'—who were writing letters in the name of Paul. For this reason, when Paul gave a letter to someone to act as a courier, he had to choose the right man or woman; someone of impeccable trust. Phoebe was probably a business woman who carried the letter to the church at Rome (Romans 16:1–2) and she was a Christian of equal trust. Paul needed agents who would not tamper with the text of his letters. In 2 Thessalonians 3:17 the apostle hints at this problem (*pseudopigraphy* is the name for this sort of thing, from two Greek words meaning 'false writing'), and he reminds the church that even if he used a scribe to write his letters for him, he always took over the quill and signed off in his own large handwriting so that they could be sure it was a letter from him: 'I, Paul, write this greeting in my own hand, which is the distinguishing mark in all my letters. This is how I write.' Earlier in the same letter he had warned the Thessalonians about prophecies, reports and letters 'supposed to have come from us' (2:2). For the same reason Paul invited the Galatians to check out his own distinctive handwriting as evidence that the letter really came from him (Galatians 6:11).

In the hands of Tychicus, Paul knew that his letter was safe: there would be no tampering with it, no changing a word here or there, or peddling it for profit among the churches. It may seem hardly likely that a true Christian would tamper with God's word by rejecting some parts here and there, but that is precisely what we can do when we downgrade Scripture by ignoring those elements that will prove unpopular, dismissing as irrelevant that which we consider to be 'culturally conditioned', and producing tortured interpretations to avoid the obvious meaning.

Paul once wrote to the Corinthians and claimed that, unlike some preachers, he would never mess with the word of God: 'Unlike so many, we do not peddle the word of God for profit. On the contrary, in Christ we speak before God with sincerity, like men sent from God' (2 Corinthians 2:17). The word *kapelos* that Paul used commonly referred to the trader, but unfortunately so many of them diluted and adulterated their goods that the word became a term to refer to the cheap and dishonest dealer. For any Christian to hold in their hand the word of God is not merely a great privilege, it is an immense responsibility: but to read it and then deny it or ignore it, is sheer dishonesty for which we will all be accountable. Tychicus could be trusted with God's word.

An honest encourager

Paul provided a slightly fuller commendation of the messenger in the letter that Tychicus carried with him back home to Asia: 'Tychicus, the dear brother and faithful servant in the Lord, will tell you everything, so that you may know how I am and what I am doing. I am sending him to you for this very purpose, that you may know how we are, and that he may encourage you'—a more literal translation is 'that he may encourage your hearts' Ephesians 6:21–22.

He is 'a dear brother'. Paul often used that kind of commendation when he was writing about people. Tychicus was not simply a man who did all the right things and could be trusted, though remaining coldly detached; he was a man of warmth and love which was reflected in the way people felt about him. He was also a 'faithful servant in the Lord'—the word 'faithful' means trustworthy and reliable—and he was a 'servant', which means that he ministered like that among the Christians.

But then notice that he would 'encourage' the Christians. This word is used of one who comes alongside to help others; it is the Greek word *paracletos*, meaning one called alongside another. The same word is used of Barnabas in Acts 4:36 when he was nicknamed 'son of encouragement'. Tychicus was an 'alongside' person; the kind of individual you love to have beside you at any time—and this was especially important in his case as we shall see shortly. Tychicus may have been one among many with this gift, but it is a definite gift from the Holy Spirit, since that is the very description we have of the Spirit himself in John 14:26.

Just occasionally a Christian will ask me how they can discover what their gift is; they say, 'I don't know that I have a spiritual gift'. My suggestion is simply this: 'Here is one that you can pray for, because it is what builds the church as much as any other: pray for the gift of encouragement.' You will find this gift listed in Romans 12:8 and Philippians 2:1.

Tychicus was a walking prayer letter from Paul: 'He will tell you everything, so that you may know how I am and what I am doing.' When Tychicus came down to the Ephesians and he brought the letter with him, an elder read it and then asked Tychicus to fill in the details and tell what God had been doing through Paul now that he was under house arrest. Paul does not tell us much about himself so they would ask, 'How is Paul, really? What is he doing? What is the pressure like in Rome and how are the Christians faring? And what about those in the household of Caesar, are they standing true, are they holding on firmly? How can we best pray for Paul and the situation there in Rome?' Doubtless they would run through a few names known to them and ask for news of them as well. They would have been interested in both the encouraging news and the discouraging news. You can imagine how another might have responded with darkness and despair: the work curtailed, Christians fearful, problems in the churches, Paul not in good health, too many false apostles around, some deserting the cause and so on. This was all sadly true, but it was not all the truth.

Tychicus, on the other hand, could be relied upon to give both good and bad news in such a way that the Christians were not discouraged. He would not let them live in glorious victory land imagining that nothing ever went wrong anywhere, nor was he going to discourage them with a message of doom and gloom. When he told them everything that was going on back in Rome, he would give them the truth, but in such a way that their hearts were encouraged. That demands a spiritual gift. It is easy to depress people and discourage them with bad news, but it is not easy to give bad news *and* encourage people at the same time. It is a great gift to encourage in a challenging way and challenge in an encouraging way. Tychicus was able to do that.

A living letter

In his commendation of Tychicus recorded in Colossians 4:7 Paul wrote much the same as in Ephesians 6:21, though with one significant difference. It is a difference that is entirely lost by most of our translations and yet it was clearly deliberate on the part of Paul. In Ephesians he refers to Tychicus as 'A dear brother and faithful servant in the Lord'; the 'servant' here translates the Greek word *diakonos* (deacon) which is used of a servant generally. However, in Colossians our translations have: 'A dear brother, faithful minister and fellow-servant'. That is very confusing and misses Paul's deliberate play with words. The 'faithful minister' is precisely the same as 'faithful servant' in Ephesians and should be translated like that; because the next phrase 'faithful servant' is altogether different: it is just one word that can best be translated 'fellow-slave'. The word *doulos* is used, and that refers to a slave. Tychicus would do anything to serve the Lord, nothing was beneath him, nothing was too humble for him to tackle. He was prepared to be less than a servant—a slave for the sake of the gospel.

But there was a more important reason why Paul chose that word 'slave' to describe Tychicus, for he was entrusted with something far more significant than either money or a letter. Sometime before, Philemon, a wealthy property owner in Colosse in whose large home the church regularly met, had come into the Christian meeting looking very angry. One of his slaves had cut and run—with some of Philemon's cash. A search revealed nothing and the slave owner never expected to see either his faithless servant or his money again. He was none too pleased. A runaway slave was always likely to put ideas into the heads of the other slaves and so he had to be particularly watchful for a while. Doubtless some of the converted slaves in the meeting felt decidedly uncomfortable as they eyed the less than happy Philemon.

In Colossians 4:9 Paul commended Tychicus and revealed who his companion was on the journey to Asia: 'He is coming with Onesimus, our faithful and dear brother, who is one of you. They will tell you everything that is happening here.' That would make everyone in the meeting place sit upright on their hard, backless stone benches—even the sleepy servant skulking on the corner seat. As he travelled to Asia, Tychicus carried in his leather pouch, three letters: one to the church at Ephesus, one to the church at Colosse, and a personal letter from Paul to Philemon.

The significance of all this, is that besides the three letters Tychicus carried with him to Colosse, he had at his side a man called Onesimus— Philemon's runaway slave! We do not know how or why, but Onesimus had found his way to Rome. Once there, perhaps he panicked; Onesimus knew the danger of being a runaway slave who had stolen or committed some other violence against his master or his master's property, and when he came to Rome he suddenly realised that he had nowhere else to go—his road ran out in the capital. At the great metropolis he had to stop running, and the only contact he knew of was a man called Paul who had often been talked about back home; his name was a household word down there in Philemon's house-church in Colosse. His story is told in the next chapter, but we can shorten it by saying that he made contact with Paul and was converted to Christ.

Shortly after Onesimus became a Christian, Paul encouraged him to return to his master. By law, branding by a hot iron on the cheek was the least that a slave master could be expected to do to a recaptured slave. Death was certainly an option. We can hear Onesimus remonstrating with Paul: 'But I can't go back, I can't face up to it; besides I haven't got any of the money left that I stole.' Excuses and reasons would come thick and fast. Onesimus knew that one thing Rome never tolerated was a slave who broke his trust, acted violently or dishonestly and ran. And Paul was now telling him he must go back and put things right. That was the very last thing that Onesimus wanted to do.

But Paul insisted: 'Onesimus, if you are going to be a Christian and you are going to be a servant of Jesus Christ and take up your cross daily and follow him, then you must start here—you must go back to your master.' Then Paul would have added, 'But it will be alright Onesimus, don't worry. Let me tell you this: Philemon was led to Christ by me just as you were. That means you go back as his brother as well as his servant: it will be alright,

Onesimus. Besides, I hope to follow as soon as I am free from this house arrest, and Philemon will know that I am on the way and he will treat you alright; he will know that I expect him to, it will be alright'. This is the emphasis of the phrase: 'Onesimus, our faithful and dear brother.' I expect Paul showed those words to the fearful slave to reassure him.

But the best reassurance of all was when Paul told Onesimus that he would not be travelling alone: 'Onesimus, I know you are still not really convinced, but you will be going along with Tychicus. Now, everybody knows Tychicus because he is a man of integrity and he is a great encourager, you will need him on the journey'. When Paul needed a man who could keep up the courage of Onesimus and his commitment to carry through what he had to do, he could have made no better choice than Tychicus. It is a great gift to be the kind of Christian others would love to have around when they are fearful of the future, trembling over their circumstances, or on a long journey for a difficult assignment.

However, I suspect Paul showed Onesimus something else in his letter to the church at Colosse. He had referred to Tychicus as a 'fellow-slave', but he deliberately did not use that word to describe Onesimus because just at the present it would have been painful even in a Christian context; he was described only as 'Our faithful and dear brother, who is one of you'. As he grew in his faith, Onesimus would come to appreciate that all the Lord's servants are in reality 'slaves' of Christ.

Can you imagine these two on the long journey—and it was a long journey—by road and sea from Rome to Colosse? They had many days together and imagine this free man with no sword in his belt taking a slave with no shackles on his legs back to his master. Here, instead, were two brothers walking, talking and praying together. Nothing quite like it had ever been seen, this was incredible. It marked a turning point in relationships in the ancient world. Christ was turning Rome upside down; stories like this just did not happen—at least they were not supposed to. This was a transformation that the first century Roman Empire had never heard about. Down through Italy, across the Mediterranean, then overland; how many times did Onesimus' faith begin to waver, but Tychicus was always there, encouraging, reassuring, stiffening his resolve. It is good to have men like that around when the going is tough and the will is weak.

But I do not believe Tychicus was sent only for the sake of Onesimus, I think he was sent to pacify Philemon as well. That was a smart move by Paul. But it had to be the right man. After all, Philemon was not a man to be trifled with. He was a property owner, perhaps with a large estate and with many other slaves. So Tychicus was there as a guarantee. When he arrived, everything was going to be alright because Tychicus was known and Tychicus would check out that Philemon treated Onesimus well.

On the substitute bench

There are only two more passing references to Tychicus in the New Testament. One is in 2 Timothy 4:12. There is a little participle here that has been omitted in some of our translations and that is unfortunate. Paul provided a list of the people who were around him in Rome and those who had left or deserted. In verse 11 he concluded, 'Only Luke is with me. Get Mark and bring him with you because he is helpful to me in my ministry. I sent Tychicus to Ephesus.' Timothy was in Ephesus and therefore there is significance in the fact that Paul had sent Tychicus to that city at the precise time he was asking that Timothy would send Mark from Ephesus.

John Mark was the first term failure who Barnabas remodelled and made useful for Paul. The apostle was humble enough, many years later, to admit that Barnabas had done a good job with John Mark and he could do with him here in Rome in these desperate days. But Timothy had his own problems in Ephesus and if he came up to Paul in Rome with John Mark, who would be left to look after the church at Ephesus? So Paul added a small but significant word in verse 12: '*But* Tychicus I sent to Ephesus...' That will make it alright. Tychicus will be a good replacement. Tychicus was always available and always valuable.

The last mention of him is in Titus 3:12 'As soon as I send Artemas or Tychicus to you (in Crete), do your best to come to me at Nicopolis, because I have decided to winter there.' Either Artemas or Tychicus would be sent to Crete, whoever returned first to Paul, so that Titus could join Paul in Rome. It is the same scenario. Titus said, 'Paul, I can't leave, who will look after the work here?' And Paul replied, 'Don't worry, either Artemas or Tychicus will be on their way.'

Tychicus was never a leader in the work like Titus or Timothy, he was never noted for his preaching like Paul or Peter or Apollos; as far as we are aware he was never a martyr for the cause of Christ like Stephen or James; he wrote no letters, planted no churches, in fact it is not recorded that he led anyone to Christ. But everywhere we meet him, he is a faithful and trustworthy servant-slave: encouraging, caring, serving. He is mentioned in despatches as one who was engaged in the spiritual battle no less than Paul himself, who fought the good fight for Jesus Christ, and who was as valuable as Timothy and Titus and any of the others for whom we have much more information. Yet we find him often sitting in reserve, waiting for a new role: a messenger entrusted with money, a vital letter, and more important than all, with a runaway slave; then on his own heading for Ephesus, or ready to accept a new post at Crete. He may not be considered for the greatest honour *here*, but who knows where Christians like this will be *there*. Never despise the role of Tychicus as an encourager, a servant-slave among God's people, someone just good to have around. The first century church was built upon little people like Tychicus and so is the church in the twenty-first century—and beyond.

Onesimus—profit and loss

'I appeal to you for my son Onesimus, who became my son while I was in chains. Formerly he was useless to you, but now he has become useful both to you and to me.' Philemon 10–11

S lavery was a widespread practice in the first century, and the entire economy of the empire depended upon it—or so it was assumed. When Paul was in Rome in the early 60s, the number of slaves amounted to around one third of the one million inhabitants in the city; a proposed law to make slaves wear a conspicuous form of dress was abandoned simply because the Senate was afraid such a move would reveal the numerical strength of the slaves and might give them ideas of their power if they banded together. However, across the empire as a whole the best conjecture is that slavery did not amount to more than twenty percent of the population. But the serviceable years of a slave were short and it probably required an annual turnover of half a million slaves to re-supply the need. Slave ownership was undoubtedly a mark of wealth and it ensured a comfortable life style; one wealthy Roman a few years before Christ's birth left over four thousand slaves in his will. However, not all the rich invested heavily in slaves; Seneca, the philosopher and ill-fated tutor to the children of Nero, was extremely wealthy and yet he took only three or four slaves with him when he travelled.

Slavery was a miserable business, and if the average age in the first century—from the evidence of tombstones—was as low as twenty to thirty years, then the lifespan of a slave could hardly be more than twenty. Slaves had virtually no legal rights. When the city Prefect, Lucius Pedanius Secundus was murdered by one of his slaves, according to law his entire household of slaves were put to death; even the Emperor was upset by this, but the law demanded it and Nero had to line the streets with soldiers as the four hundred men, women and children were led to their execution. And that was in Rome in the year AD 61, just two years before Paul wrote this letter to Philemon from the same city. But much depended upon how a man came into slavery.

One of the most fruitful sources of slavery was through prisoners of war—the contemporary Jewish historian Josephus put the number of Jews sold into slavery after the uprising and destruction of Jerusalem in AD 70 as ninety-seven thousand—and many of the armies in the first century were followed by slave traders who bought prisoners from them to trade in the slave market. During the first century, a regular supply of slaves came from the newly conquered territory of Britannia Romana. Piracy and kidnapping also added to the pool, though with recent successes against the Mediterranean pirates these sources were clearly insufficient. A man or woman could become a slave as a result of criminal activity or debt, and another major source must have been slaves born into that condition, since the law stipulated that the child of a slave was automatically a slave; although with probably three quarters of the slaves being men this would hardly supply sufficient replacements! Others were sold into slavery by their parents in order to raise cash in times of hardship. However, some historians believe that a significant source was from unwanted offspring thrown out to die who were 'rescued from the dung-pile for enslavement'— there is plenty of contemporary evidence that this 'child-exposure' was commonplace at this time.

A profitable slave

Just how Onesimus came into slavery or what kind of slave he was we are not told, but there is at least one significant clue, and that is his name. 'Onesimus' means 'profitable' or 'useful'. It could have been given him by an over eager father with an eye on the future value of an extra hand on the family farm. However I think it is more likely that he was given this name either when he was born into slavery or when he came into the household of Philemon as an anonymous worker picked up in the slave market. His only value was to be a useful slave and his only significance in life was as an implement of labour, nothing more.

Life for slaves was always hard and frequently dreary and monotonous. Some slaves formed societies, which they called *collegia*, to encourage each other for what one historian refers to as 'protection against oppression, for mutual sympathy and support, for relief from the deadly dullness of an obscure and sordid life.'

All this is the background to the enormity of this man's crime before his conversion. Second only to murder was the slave who stole and ran—that was Onesimus. In verse 11 Paul may be doing more than playing with his name Onesimus; it reads: 'Formerly he was useless to you, but now he has become useful both to you and to me.' Perhaps Paul was summarising his life as a slave. He was a useless slave and Philemon was fed up with him; what annoyed him above all was that Onesimus stole before he left. In verse 18 there is a strong hint of theft: 'If he has done you any wrong or owes you anything charge it to me.' Paul evidently knew exactly what he had done because Onesimus told Paul everything. He doubtless knew the amount, but he would not include this in his letter because that would expose Onesimus to the eyes of any who got sight of this letter to Philemon; Paul would leave it to the runaway slave to own up to his master.

That crime of stealing and escaping gave the master the right to execute his slave if he was caught, or at least to brand him on the cheek with a hot iron so that forever to his dying day he would be known as a runaway slave. Some slaves wore a little tag that declared: 'If you find me, return me to my master.' And here was Paul sending him back, nine hundred miles as the stork flies, from Rome to Colosse. Not in chains but with a friend and brother in Christ, Tychicus. It is hard for us in the twenty-first century to understand how revolutionary that was. No other society in the first century Roman Empire could handle the situation like this.

Just how unusual this was, can be understood by the way Paul prepared the ground. He was almost halfway through his letter before he came to the real reason for writing: 'I appeal to you for my son Onesimus, who became my son whilst I was in chains' (v 10). But see how Paul edged into the subject from verses 7–9. He began by telling Philemon how encouraged he was by the love and encouragement Philemon had shown to everyone. That is the preparation for continuing, 'Now you will encourage me, won't you, Philemon? I expect you to do exactly what I will ask of you. I haven't told you what it is yet, but when I tell you I expect you to agree.' Then Paul built his argument: 'I want you to remember that I am Paul the apostle, and please respect the seniority of my age, and do not forget that I am a prisoner—and that you owe your own spiritual life to me.' Only now was Paul ready to make his appeal—but it was virtually an unanswerable case by the time he arrived at his conclusion.

Refuge in Rome

It is intriguing to speculate how Onesimus discovered Paul in Rome. According to the apostle, Onesiphorus would later have great difficulty finding the apostle in the same city (2 Timothy 1:17) and *he* was not a runaway slave who had to keep a low profile. Perhaps Onesimus fled to Rome in order to lose himself in the great metropolis and, having arrived, he soon spent Philemon's money and then panicked. What could he do now? Where could he turn? He could hardly go down to the slave market and sell himself all over again—he might end up with Philemon a second time! Doubtless Onesimus had heard of Paul and the gospel. Maybe he had been to some of the meetings in Philemon's home, and so he set out to find this man who was such big news in the congregation at Colosse. He had never seen or heard Paul, because Colosse had never been visited by the apostle.

However it came about, the fugitive slave discovered where Paul was under house arrest and it was not long before he had come to understand Paul's gospel and handed his life over to Christ. Whether Paul was on trial before a local governor or the Roman Emperor, or whether he was chatting to the sentry on guard at his door or listening to the story of a worthless slave, Paul had no different gospel. He would tell the same message to whoever was in front of him. There is only one gospel and it suits every man, woman and child from every and any station in life, in every culture and in every age. It is the gospel of the saving grace of a Saviour who died on the cross that we might be forgiven; who carried our sin and our guilt and our penalty upon himself so that he could take everything we deserve and give us everything we do not deserve. Onesimus heard all this. And for the first time Onesimus felt valued and he responded to the truth of the gospel.

But how was Paul sure that Onesimus was really converted? After all, the man was in a fix, to put it mildly. He was in big trouble and the future did not look at all bright; one false move would discover him as a runaway slave and he could expect little mercy. He could give himself up, or starve or steal.

There were few options left for him. So, how easy it would be to make a profession of faith and rely on Paul to sort it out with Philemon. What were the marks of real conversion in this man's life? Paul can tell us that.

First of all, he had owned up to his past. Paul knew very well what he had done: he had stolen and whatever else, and he had described himself in such negative terms that Paul had come to the conclusion that Onesimus had been a pretty useless slave. Paul wrote as much to Philemon: 'He was useless to you' (v 11). The tense implies that Onesimus was worthless even before he ran—and nobody argued with that. Onesimus did not protest that he was no more useless than Philemon was before *his* conversion. Nor did he avoid the issue by referring to the severity of his treatment as a slave and the unfairness of it all; or that there were far worse slaves than him in the *collegia*. Certainly there are some sins that are more serious than others, and that is why there are grades of punishment, but there are no sins that cannot be forgiven by God—and no sins that do not need to be forgiven by God. Onesimus gave evidence that he understood all this.

The one thing that marked out this man Onesimus was that he owned up to it all. I imagine he sat down with Paul and said, 'You might as well know the kind of person I was, and Philemon does not know the half of it.' Then Paul would say something like this: 'Onesimus, I want to tell you something about Philemon: when I first met him he was just like you. Oh, he was not a slave, he was a free man, and he was pretty well off. But he was no more and no less in chains than you, Onesimus. He was a slave to sin, because the one thing he could do without trying was to sin and the one thing he could not do, however hard he tried, was to stop sinning. So, Onesimus, there was no difference between you and Philemon.'

Knowing Christ begins with an admission of personal guilt and uselessness to God. Until we come to that point, there is no Christianity and no hope of salvation. Christ came to call sinners to repentance, not the self-righteous. Repentance is when all the defences come down and we admit that we are useless in the sight of God; we do not compare ourselves with others, or plead the excuse of our background, our problems, our difficulties, our broken home, or our upbringing. We simply admit that we are useless in the sight of God—we are sinners.

But another reason why Paul had no doubt that this man was truly converted was that he had proved himself valuable: 'Now he has become useful both to you and to me … I would have liked to keep him with me so that he could take your place in helping me while I am in chains for the gospel' (vs 11,13). At last he lived up to his name: Onesimus—'useful'. The word that Paul used in v 13 of the service he would like to retain from Onesimus is the word *diaconos* which means 'servant' not 'slave'. That was a gentle touch from Paul by avoiding the word 'slave' that legally defined him; he did not use *diaconos* in a formal sense of the word, it was simply a description of his willingness to serve as a Christian.

In 2 Timothy 2:20–21 we have an illustration that Onesimus would easily have understood, and perhaps Paul used it first to help this converted slave understand his new role in life: 'In a large house there are articles not only of gold and silver, but also of wood and clay; some are for noble purposes and some for ignoble. If a man cleanses himself from the latter, he will be an instrument for noble purposes, made holy, useful to the master and prepared to do any good work.' Onesimus knew all about that. A trusted servant cleaned the gold and silver; other servants slopped out the latrines and the kitchen waste bins. Onesimus stole the first because he was probably fed up cleaning the second—and then he ran!

Imagine Paul talking through that picture with him as he introduced the gospel: 'Onesimus, do you want to go on being rubbish or do you want to be useful for God? It is not the container that is dishonourable but what it contains that marks the whole thing as either clean or dirty. You can have a wooden fruit bowl and you can have a silver rubbish bin. Onesimus, God's servants may not all be silver but they must all be clean. Do you want to be useful to a new master? No, I am not talking now about Philemon, I am talking about the best and kindest Master you could ever have. Then you must be clean and you must show yourself useful.' Interestingly, the same word that Paul used in 2 Timothy 2:21, '*useful* to the master', is precisely the word that is used here in verse 11 when he is writing to Philemon: '*useful* to you and me'. And in Philemon 11, the same play on the words 'useless' and 'useful' comes over in Paul's Greek: *achrestos* and *euchrestos*

'Useful to you and me'. Paul expected consistency in this man because he knew that he was a trusted man. He had already kept him in Rome long enough to test him out, and Onesimus could have run again, but he didn't.

Perhaps Paul introduced him to a Christian home somewhere in the city, and each day he would come into Paul's room and listen again as the apostle explained the gospel and helped him to understand his Christian faith. The evidence of conversion is a changed life and consistent behaviour. There is no conversion without a changed life.

There is an odd idea of what conversion is today: so long as someone makes a profession of faith we are quite satisfied—we have a statistic. But heaven is not fooled by that; when the angels rejoice over a sinner who repents, they know who truly has repented and who has not, and thus they know when to rejoice and when not to rejoice. The enthusiasm and diligence of this man without any rights, and who could have been picked up by any Roman soldier and sold into the slave market, convinced Paul that the converted slave was genuine. Onesimus was never taught by Paul that Christianity came in two distinct packages: first, you take Christ as Saviour, and then later you may take Christ as Lord. Paul offered him all or nothing.

However, the greatest test of Onesimus' new birth was just about to come. Imagine another of Paul's conversations with him:

'Onesimus you are a brother in Christ.'

'That's wonderful Paul, nobody has ever called me a brother before.'

'Well I'm telling you now. You are a brother in Christ; in fact, Onesimus, you are my brother. You have heard the story of how I became a Christian. You know that I was a Jewish teacher; I had a good education at the university. But, Onesimus, those things I count as rubbish in the light of the value of knowing Christ. Now you may not have the same background as me, but you're my brother.'

'Well that's great Paul, I'm so glad to be your brother.'

'More than that, Onesimus, Epaphroditus is your brother as well, and so is Tychicus. And you are the brother of all the brothers and sisters in the church at Rome—and beyond.'

'That's tremendous Paul; I'm part of a great family all over the world?'

'That's right Onesimus. And that means you are Philemon's brother.'

'Ah, that's good too. But I'm glad he is a long way off; let's hope he's a nice brother if he gets to hear about all this.'

'Oh, he'll get to know alright.'

'How's that then?'

'Because, Onesimus, you are going to tell him!'

Perhaps Onesimus half guessed this was coming. In the absence of mobiles, text messages and e-mails, he knew that there was only one conclusion. It meant that he would have to return to Colosse and meet his old master face to face. That was the legal and proper thing to do; Paul would be breaking Roman law to harbour this illegal immigrant in the metropolis! But Paul softened the blow for him. He told him that one of the most trusted men in the city church would accompany him on that journey, to keep up his courage, vouch for his passage should anyone suspect him as a runaway, and to ensure that all would be well in Colosse. That man was Tychicus.

I doubt that there was any other runaway slave in the first century who had returned to his master in the way Onesimus went back to his. Not in chains but with his friend and brother Tychicus beside him—that trusted encourager-friend. There must have been times on that long haul back to Colosse when the confidence and courage of Onesimus was failing him and he would plead, 'Tychicus, do we have to go on? Can't we just stop off here? It's a long way.' And Tychicus would reply: 'Come on. This is a part of your new life, and you are going to see what God does and how God changes relationships. I will show you something, Onesimus, that you never thought was possible, and we are going to trust that God will work it out right.'

Christ gives a new perspective on our past

Significantly, Paul was careful to make sure that both Onesimus and Philemon should learn to view their past through Christian eyes. The telling explanation in Philemon 15–16 is quite deliberate: 'Perhaps the reason he was separated from you for a little while was that you might have him back for good—no longer as a slave, but better than a slave, as a dear brother.' At the time of the departure of this worthless slave, Philemon could see no good purpose in it: he had lost a slave, money, perhaps credibility among the Christians (what kind of master was he if his slaves ran away?), and authority among his other slaves (it never looked good if a slave owner could not keep his household in order). For his part, Onesimus could not see anything good in his life up until now. By whatever means he came into slavery, it was hardly the preferred lifestyle of those with free choice: remember 'the deadly dullness of an obscure and sordid life'?

But now each man must see things very differently. 'Was separated' is hardly the way Onesimus saw it, he could not get away fast enough and had no intention of returning; Philemon would not think this word appropriate since it was used of a divorce! But that is how they must now view it. This is what later theologians would call 'prevenient grace'—the kind providence of God in our lives long before we reach out for him; indeed the providence that makes us reach out for him, and the grace that goes before us (that's the meaning of the old word 'prevenient') in every step of our way through life.

The phrase 'perhaps the reason' in Philemon 15 is something of a paraphrase of just one word. The word Paul used can be translated either as 'perhaps' or 'quickly'—the context generally decides, and in this case it could be either. Maybe Paul was referring to the hasty exit of Onesimus from the household: 'For he left in a hurry just for a little while.' The 'little while' was certainly not the slave's intention, but it was God's! The phrase 'for a little while' is a free rendering of two words that are literally 'for an hour'. Since the hour was almost the shortest measurement of time reasonably possible in the first century, the word for 'hour' came to be used for our expression 'in just a minute' or 'in a moment'. In other words, what you intended to be a forever break was in reality to be a forever reunion. But more of that in a moment. How great are the prevenient plans of a providential God. Every Christian should have a new perspective on the past. This, of course, is precisely how Joseph viewed his cruel slavery in Egypt nineteen hundred years earlier: 'It was not you who sent me here, but God' (Genesis 45:8).

Christ gives a new perspective on our present

Here was the tremendous privilege of conversion. God does not break down all the structures of society but he breaks down the barriers of society. Onesimus was going back to serve Philemon, even as a slave, but there was a new relationship between the two men. And in the first century Roman Empire that would not be easy to work out—but work it out they must. His legal status would be the same but his relationship and his service would be radically different.

In Colossians 4:9 Paul commended Onesimus to the whole church; this letter accompanied the personal letter to Philemon and it was important that the whole church was aware of Paul's estimate of the converted slave. That would put even more pressure on Philemon! Incidentally, it is a mark of Philemon's compliance and humility that we have his personal letter at all; it would have been all too easy for Philemon to have kept that letter to himself and for it never to have been read by millions of Christians over the next two thousand years; of course it is possible that Paul was sufficiently cautious to furnish Tychicus with a 'spare copy' that he later released for general interest. But I prefer the first explanation as being more in keeping with the kind of man we can believe Philemon was—eager to let the church learn valuable lessons, even at his own expense.

Paul referred to Onesimus as 'Our faithful and dear brother, who is one of you.' Paul wanted the church to realise that when Onesimus came among them, he was just like everybody else. The moment he walked through the doors of the meeting place, especially if it was in Philemon's house, there would be no distinctions. He would sit where he wished and be accepted as a brother. Philemon himself would be offered no better seat. In fact, may we believe that here in the Christian congregation Philemon and Onesimus could sit side by side on the first Sunday after the renegade's return?

For his part, Philemon was reminded that Tychicus is 'better than a slave, a dear brother' (Philemon 16). That took some swallowing even for Philemon! In more ways than one, Onesimus had proved to be a very costly investment, but now, if we may coin a pun in the English that is not there in the Greek, he was to be 'even dearer'! More than this, if Philemon considered Paul to be a partner in the gospel, then he must think of Onesimus in just the same way (v 17). But Paul had set an exquisite example of his trust in Onesimus in his letter to the whole church: the apostle deliberately linked Onesimus with Tychicus as the two men entrusted with the news from Rome '*They* will tell you everything that is happening here' (Colossians 4:9). What an encouragement to this once useless slave to be honoured with such trust from the great apostle himself. Paul knew how to make a young Christian feel good!

However, none of this would allow Onesimus to take advantage of his new relationship with his owner. Doubtless he had already had the benefit of the advice that Paul would later set down to Timothy for the instruction of the Christian slaves at Ephesus. He must consider his master as 'worthy of full respect'; and because Philemon is a Christian, he must not show less respect for Onesimus because he is a brother, instead, he is to serve 'even better' because the one who benefits from his service is a believer and therefore 'dear to them' (1 Timothy 6:2).

Paul was well aware how the servants talked about their masters at the end of a weary day of labour; it would not be easy for Onesimus to hold back from that conversation. Nor would it be easy for him to resist the temptation to steal and boast of his successes as he used to. It was certainly all change for everyone. And in the first century it was radical change. But the application is no less real and decisive in the twenty-first century.

Paul was not demolishing the structure but was altering the relationship in society—there is a difference. That is why the New Testament always recognises leadership in every part of society: in the state, in industry, in the church and in the family. This is God's pattern for a fallen world. The New Testament never refers to a society in which all are equal in authority, but it clearly insists that all are equal in value. That is a vital distinction. Galatians 3:28 is a false charter for many: 'There is neither Jew nor Greek, slave nor free, male nor female, for you are all one in Christ Jesus.' From this one verse a completely unbiblical imbalance is drawn that everyone in Christ is equal in every way. That is not what Paul is saying, and 1 Timothy 6:2 makes the position clear. There is a distinction between the master and the slave. The one has authority over the other. It is the same in the state, in industry, in the church and in the family. Onesimus would now find his true value and fulfilment, not in his work or status as a slave, but in his value to Christ.

Thinking of the family inevitably leads us to Ephesians 5:22–28 where the authority and subjection of husband and wife are in the context of love, dignity and value. That is true Christianity. The world says submission means inferiority and authority means superiority. But submission to authority does not mean inferiority. The gospel has an unpleasant way of turning our patterns the other way round. Could it be possible that at some time in the future Onesimus may have become an elder in the church—and Philemon may not? Now *there* would be a problem for the early church to sort out!

Christ gives a new perspective on our future

It is disappointing that some translators have rendered Philemon 15 like this: 'Perhaps the reason he was separated from you for a little while was that you might have him back for good.' That implies that Philemon would have his slave back for the better, which of course was true, but that is not what Paul meant. The word he used means 'for ever'. That is a far bigger claim. Paul is not counting the denarius value of this new-made slave, but his eternal value. Paul was playing on the two contrasts: 'a little while' (*hora*) and 'for ever' (*aionios*).

Philemon might look on his servants as his property until they die, but here is at least one that he will have for all eternity. Not as a slave, but as a brother. They will be serving God together for ever. In fact, it is the only relationship that lasts for ever. And that is something the world cannot match or understand. Apart from Christ, death ends all relationships. But in Christ all things are new and all things are for ever. By contrast, the ancient Egyptians made little models of their servants, placed them in their tombs, and expected them to come to life in the other world to carry on their service. There would be a far better relationship between these two men than that.

Step into the sandals of Onesimus for a moment. See what a glorious future this was for the man who had no future, who did not even know his past and who lived a poor, miserable and mundane present. Suddenly he is converted and all his relationships change: the way he views his past, present and his future is radically new. Now he has a future, a hope and an eternal Kingdom to look forward to. I am sure that when, back in Rome, Onesimus questioned Paul as to how the apostle could be so calm in face of the threat of death constantly hanging over him, he received the same assurance that was given to the Corinthians: 'We know that if the earthly tent we live in is destroyed, we have a building from God, an eternal house in heaven' (2 Corinthians 5:1). Onesimus would have been reassured that he was now a 'for ever' person and all his relationships in Christ would be for ever.

One day we can enquire into the conclusion of the incredible story of one of God's little people that so transformed relationships in the first century Roman empire.

Onesiphorus—a pastor for Paul

'May the Lord show mercy to the household of Onesiphorus, because he often refreshed me and was not ashamed of my chains. On the contrary, when he was in Rome, he searched hard for me until he found me. May the Lord grant that he will find mercy from the Lord on that day! You know very well in how many ways he helped me in Ephesus' 2 Timothy 1:16–18.

Some Christians were finding Paul an embarrassment. He was too dangerous, too energetic, too uncompromising—and now he had landed himself in prison. It all began five or six years ago with a riot in Jerusalem back in AD 59 and since then Paul had never been a free man, moving from house arrest to prison.

The story started in Acts 21 when Paul's actions stirred up the mob in Jerusalem. Perhaps we cannot blame Paul for the riot, but he did not exactly poor oil on troubled waters; in fact he threw it on the flames! When the Roman soldiers rescued him from the riotous mob and brought him into the barracks, Paul could have kept quiet, but instead he asked permission of the commander to stand up and address the crowd: his testimony infuriated them.

Many of the Christians thought that if only Paul had kept his head down, the rabble would have lost interest—but he didn't. Then, after two years in prison, just at the moment when the governor thought it was safe to release him, Paul appealed to Caesar. Why, O why? That was just asking for trouble. Didn't Paul realise that the Emperor Nero—'the mad butcher of Rome'—was hardly likely to be favourable to an upstart religion that threatened the stability of the Empire with its insistence upon recognising Jesus as King? Who, in their right mind, would appeal for justice to Nero? All the Christians knew that Paul wanted to visit Rome, he said so in his letters, but there were more straightforward ways of getting there.

Admittedly it meant that the Romans paid his fare, but look at the predicament he was now in: nothing but law courts and trials—and worse. Some concluded that Paul was his own worst enemy. If only he would lie low for a bit, keep out of trouble and let things die down; maybe compromise a little here and there and tone down the exclusive message that Christ is the only way. But he would have none of this, and those around him would inevitably get sucked in. So, some decided that the best course of action was to distance themselves from him and wait and see how things turned out. As a result, when Paul picked up his pen to write what is possibly his last letter (2 Timothy), it was a sad story that he related. He felt deserted by all the Christians in the province of Asia, 'including Phygelus and Hermogenes' (1:15) whose withdrawal was clearly both a surprise and a great disappointment. At the end of the letter Paul picked up the same theme: when he stood on trial at his first court appearance before the Emperor he stood alone. Demas has deserted him (4:10), but he was not the only one; it seemed that everyone had disappeared (v 16) and the prisoner felt as alone as if this was his Gethsemane. Some who might have stood by him, like Crescens, Titus and Tychicus, had been sent off on mission to various cities, and in their absence, Alexander the blacksmith was making life especially hard for Paul (4:14), and Hymenaeus and Philetus were spreading heresy (2:17)—though whether in Rome or at Ephesus Paul does not say.

It is hardly surprising that the apostle kept reminding Timothy, the young pastor at Ephesus, that he was engaged in a battle: 'Endure hardship with us like a good soldier of Jesus Christ' (2:3). Paul's life was certainly not one upwardly mobile story of success. The greatest burden he had to carry was the disloyalty, carelessness, opposition and error of so-called Christian workers. Here, at the end of his life, in chains, in prison and facing death by execution at any time, Paul felt abandoned and alone. Almost pathetically he wrote to Timothy pleading for loyalty: Timothy please don't be ashamed of the gospel and don't be ashamed of my chains either. Many are, but Timothy don't you join them; stand by me Timothy, because I need your support (1:7–8).

However, Paul was not as abandoned as he felt, and in reality he knew it. Not only did the Lord stand beside him (4:17), but there were many Christians who had not deserted him either, and among these was a man called Onesiphorus, who will always best be known as Paul's pastor.

Chapter 5

The Great Fire of Rome

There was never any doubt that Paul had his low times on mission and in prison. He reminded the Corinthians that in Asia he was so utterly unbearably crushed that he even despaired of life (2 Corinthians 1:8). He wrote of being forsaken and cast down. And here in Rome in AD 64, persecution was rising and Christians were scattering. Paul was trying to keep in touch with his Christian soldiers across the Empire from his prison cell but it was not easy. Some were deserting, others were taken into custody, and the church was under great pressure; Paul worried about them as any caring pastor and leader would. He brought them to the Lord but he did not find it easy to leave them there: Are they standing firm? Are the leaders holding on? Are they falling into error? Paul found himself weighed down in prison by the constant shifting problems—and then disaster struck.

On 18 June AD 64 the centre of Rome burned. To this day we cannot be sure who started the fire. Rumour quickly spread that Nero had arranged it in order to clear out the grubby city centre and make way for a brand new plan including some fine buildings and his own magnificent golden house. He wanted to create a brown field site for urban redevelopment. Whoever was responsible, a large area of the city was destroyed. In the following chaos and rumour we may assume that the Christians were finding it difficult not only to meet together, but to keep in touch with each other. Prisoners had to be moved around, and somehow they lost contact with Paul. What was even worse, was the fact that Nero spread a malicious rumour that the Christians were responsible for the fire, and in the streets of Rome the cry went up: 'Christians to the lions'.

Cornelius Tacitus was a Roman lawyer, consul and historian who was just four years old at the time of the fire. Writing in his *annals* of the Emperors from Augustus to Nero, he reports on the rumour that Nero himself had started the fire—Tacitus clearly believed Nero was responsible:

And so, to get rid of this rumour, Nero set up as the culprits and punished with the utmost refinement of cruelty a class hated for their abominations, who are commonly called Christians. Chrèstus, from whom their name is derived, was executed at the hands of the procurator Pontius Pilate in the reign of Tiberius ... Accordingly, arrest was first made of those who confessed [to being Christians]; then, on their evidence, an immense multitude was convicted, not so much on the charge of arson as because of hatred of the human race. Besides being put to death they were made to serve as objects of amusement; they were clad in the hides of beasts and torn to death by dogs; others were crucified, others set on fire to serve to illuminate the night when daylight failed. Nero had thrown open his grounds for the display, and was putting on a show in the circus, where he mingled with the people in the dress of a charioteer or drove about in his chariot.

Tacitus commented that eventually this even gave rise to pity for the Christians, not because they did not deserve punishment, but because it was all 'to gratify the cruelty of an individual.' Another historian, Gaius Suetonius, writing around the same time, comments on the persecutions under Nero in AD 64: 'Punishment was inflicted on the Christians, a set of men adhering to a novel and mischievous superstition.'

It was a dangerous and volatile time: the attitude of the jailers was changing and conditions were getting worse and more uncomfortable. Christians could not be sure who to trust, and under the pressure of sadistic torture some were betraying their brothers and sisters in Christ; unconverted relatives were happy to keep on the right side of the law and inform on those who were meeting secretly. There is a tragic and telling plea from Paul to Timothy in 4:13, that if Timothy is able to get to Rome (perhaps if his courage does not fail him?) there are a few belongings Paul would like him to bring: 'When you come, bring the cloak that I left with Carpus at Troas, and my scrolls, especially the parchments.' In spite of the dangers and imminent threat of death, Paul must get on with his work.

This is reminiscent of the only known letter of William Tyndale, the Reformer and translator who gave us our first printed New Testament in English. The letter was written from his cell in the grim Castle of Vilvorde in Belgium shortly before his own execution in October 1536. Tyndale was suffering from the bitter cold of the winter of 1535/36 and part of the letter he wrote to the governor of the prison reads like this:

'I beg your lordship and that by Jesus Christ, that if I am to remain here through the winter you will request the commissary to have the kindness to send me from the goods of mine which he has, a warmer cap for I suffer greatly from cold in the head and am afflicted by perpetual catarrh which is much increased in this cell. A warmer coat also, for this one which I have is very thin, a piece of cloth too to patch my leggings. My overcoat is worn out; my shirt is also worn out. He has a woollen shirt if he will be good enough to send it. I also have with him leggings of thicker cloth to put on above. He also has warmer caps. And I ask to be allowed to have a lamp in the evening it is indeed wearisome sitting alone in the dark. But most of all I beg and beseech your clemency to be urgent with the commissary that he will kindly permit me to have a Hebrew Bible, Hebrew grammar and Hebrew dictionary that I may pass the time in that study. In return may you obtain what you most desire so only that it be for the salvation of your soul.'

Fifteen hundred years earlier, another prisoner waiting for execution asked for nothing more or less: warmer clothes and books. Two men in prison, two men determined they will use their time wisely for God and they will allow no opportunity to pass. Two men at the end of their lives both about the same distance away from their execution, two men resolute that they will be in harness for God until the very end.

Enter Onesiphorus!

At these times of discouragement, despondency and danger, one man stood out above all as a great encouragement, his name was Onesiphorus which, by a nice coincidence means, 'bringer of help'—though his parents could not have known how suitable that was when they gave it to him as a baby.

However, more important than what he was called is what he did. Paul says 'he often refreshed me'. That is a powerful word that is rarely used in the New Testament. The verb is used only here, but you will find the noun in Acts 3:19. Peter was preaching, and in the course of his sermon he had been telling people not only how they can become Christians, but what God has promised for the church of Christ into the future. God has promised 'times of refreshing' that will come to the church before Christ returns in glory. The verb means to recreate or revive; it carries the idea of breathing into something to give it life. Peter's use of the noun is a promise for times of spiritual revival.

When Onesiphorus walked into Paul's prison cell it was like a breath of fresh air. The apostle felt recreated, rejuvenated, spiritually revived. It is a great gift to be able to move among others, sit down alongside them, talk with them—casually or seriously—and always to bring into their life a sense of the reality of God that leaves them feeling revived. That was Onesiphorus.

But how did Onesiphorus achieve this? I believe it was what he did not talk about as much as what he did talk about and what he was rather than what he brought. I do not think that Onesiphorus allowed Paul endlessly to talk about the deserters Demas, Phygelus and Hermogenes or the gangrenous Hymenaeus and Philetus, or the heavy handed Alexander the metalworker. I can imagine that when Onesiphorus came in and joined Paul there were times when he found the apostle focussing on all who had abandoned him and who had failed the gospel. But Onesiphorus would say: 'Paul, don't get hung up on them. I know how you feel, but let's not talk about them all the time, that will only discourage us, let us keep our eyes on something bigger and our conversation on something better.'

When professing Christians turn their back on the gospel, abandon the family of God, or criticise and oppose their leaders, they do more damage then they will ever realise; they distract Christians from the real task. When Paul brooded over Demas, Phygelus, Hermogenes, Alexander, Hymenaeus and Philetus, it made him sad, angry and worried. But when Onesiphorus came in he turned Paul's mind away to better things.

I do not think Onesiphorus spent hours talking about the ailments of his family either. He had a family back in Ephesus and I have no doubt that when he came into the prison, one of the first questions Paul would have asked was: 'Onesiphorus how lovely to see you, how are you? How is the family?' Can you imagine that Onesiphorus was the sort of man to respond, 'Well Paul, since you ask, I have been suffering from incredible headaches recently and I feel thoroughly depressed; and Paul, since you ask about the family, well my wife's arthritis has got worse and worse and the kids are quite unbearable, and they are not getting on very well at school. And you should hear what's going on in the church at Ephesus! Everything seems to be going wrong down there; they have lost their love for Christ, there is a spiritual coldness about the place and there is a lot of bad teaching going on. Paul, you are better off here, because down there in Ephesus it is really miserable.' That is the kind of response Paul could expect from many Christians.

So what did Onesiphorus do? In order to revive Paul's drooping spirit they must have talked of Christ. Nothing would have revived Paul better than that. He must have sat down with Paul and talked about the life and the death, the resurrection and the return in glory of Christ; he would have refreshed Paul by a reminder of the greatness of his salvation and the glory of the gospel. He would have encouraged Paul by reminding him that he was where he was because of his faithfulness to the gospel, and more than that, he would have reminded Paul of a God who was absolutely sovereign and who worked everything for good for those who love him. But did Paul not know all this? Of course he did, but Onesiphorus was not afraid to remind even the great apostle of what he needed to hold on to. He would also have encouraged Paul by asking him how best he could pray for him. One of my memorable encouragements was when a deacon came to me in the entrance lobby one Sunday morning and asked quietly and simply: 'Brian, what can I pray for you?'

Now supposing we had been Paul's pastor, how many of us would have found ourselves thinking like this: 'What on earth can I say to the apostle Paul? Who do I think I am? He has travelled the empire with the gospel, he has written these magnificently spiritual and inspired letters, he has given us the word of God; what can I say to encourage him?' Onesiphorus was a Christian worker who loved Christ and talked easily and naturally about his Saviour, he did not despise the gift that is referred to in Romans 12:8 as the gift of encouraging. The importance of that gift is that the word for 'encourage' is the word that is used to describe the work of the Holy Spirit, that is why he is sometimes called the 'paraclete'. It refers to someone who is called alongside to help someone else. So just as the Holy Spirit is called alongside to help us, so those who have the gift of encouragement are given the gift of being called alongside others to encourage them; they are the gift of the Holy Spirit moving through them and in them alongside others. So the gift of encouragement is doing the Holy Spirit's work among the church. That cannot be unimportant.

But let me show you how else Onesiphorus was such an encouragement to Paul.

First. Onesiphorus was not ashamed of Paul

There is great significance in the phrase: 'He was not ashamed of my chains' (1:16). Many were! We are living at the safe distance of nearly two thousand years from where Paul was lying in a Roman prison. But those were very dangerous days for the Christians, and Paul must have been more than anxious for the young converts who so soon were going to face cruel persecution. Onesiphorus did not visit Paul to gain some kind of kudos by being able to tell all the Christians how he had visited the apostle. There was no kudos in being a Christian or visiting Paul. Many were abandoning Paul or at least keeping their distance.

Imagine Onesiphorus for a moment at the gate of the prison. He has called to see a prisoner and the guard on duty responds: 'Who? Paul? Oh him. That funny little religious fanatic; you one of 'im are you? Don't waste your time, they are going to top 'im any day now. He doesn't get as many visitors as he used to you know. This Christian thing is fizzling out, didn't you know that? Hasn't had a visitor for a while now.'

But Onesiphorus was insistent. Perhaps the Christians were even treating Onesiphorus with caution because he was so regularly visiting Paul. There are Christians in our churches who are never invited into the homes of others and lonely believers who are never visited. Few care whether they encourage them or not. Most are concerned only for friendships that do them good and advance their reputation. Onesiphorus was such an encouragement to Paul because he was not ashamed of him, when some Christians were.

Secondly. Onesiphorus was persistent

Paul tells us that Onesiphorus searched hard until he found him. I can only conjecture why it was so difficult to find Paul in Rome, but clearly it was. Perhaps it says something about how few Christians were visiting Paul at this time, or more likely how difficult it was to locate him or get permission to visit him. Perhaps, quite genuinely, many of the Christians just did not know where Paul was. There had been massive upheavals in Rome; prisoners were being moved around and the Christians were being blamed for the fire. It was the worst possible time to go and ask an official where Paul was! You can almost hear Paul's exclamation of grateful surprise in his letter. He writes, 'He searched hard for me'—and the little word 'until' that follows has been inserted by our translators, but if you leave it out, you can hear the exclamation: 'He searched hard for me—and he found me!'. Not everybody found Paul, not everybody wanted to find him, not everybody searched hard for him. Even some of those who searched hard did not find him. And perhaps some of those whom Paul thought had deserted him had simply given up any hope of finding him.

It was the dogged perseverance of Onesiphorus that encouraged Paul as much as anything. The word Paul used is that his friend searched 'diligently, eagerly', it carries the idea of enthusiasm and zeal. This man was not half hearted in his search. He was not eager to get back to the relative security of home and claim that he tried to find Paul but things were so chaotic in Rome that he had to give up. Peter used the same word in 2 Peter 1:5,15 where it is translated 'make every effort'. It is not always *what* we do that is such an encouragement to others but *how* we do it. Our personal sacrifice, our sheer perseverance, our faithful continuing, is always an encouragement to others.

According to Paul 'He often refreshed me'. He came back again and again. It was not just one quick visit and back to Ephesus. Here was a man who knew how important it was to encourage Paul, and he knew what it took to encourage him. Sadly many Christians today have lost that sense of responsibility to be a *reliable and persistent* encouragement. Paul could rely upon Onesiphorus to come back—and he always did.

Encouragers are those who have read Colossians 3:23 and take it seriously: 'Whatever you do, work at it with all your heart, as working for the Lord, not for men.' Or Ecclesiastes 9:10, 'Whatever your hand finds to do, do it with all your might.' This was all the more commendable because Onesiphorus was a family man, the apostle makes that clear in v 16, 'may the Lord show mercy to the household of Onesiphorus', and this is picked up again in 4:19. Some Christians neglect their families for the work of the gospel and some Christians neglect the work of the gospel for their families—neither is keeping in step with the Spirit. But Jesus was right when he warned that a man's enemies will be the members of his own household. Onesiphorus was prepared to leave his family behind in order to do a greater ministry and visit Paul. He was not so bound up with his own family that he neglected the members of the household of faith.

The reason why Paul twice refers to the 'household' of Onesiphorus is that he knew the cost to them for Paul to have the benefit of the company of the head of the household. It was not easy for the family to accept the absence of Onesiphorus in these days, and to know that he was hazarding his own freedom and even his life in order to bring encouragement to Paul. Ever the caring pastor, Paul did not overlook this cost shared by the whole family. The history of the Christian church is littered with the tragedies of families destroyed by a zealous father who neglected them for what he considered to be 'more important' matters. Paul was as carefully guarding the household of Onesiphorus, as the man himself was looking after the apostle.

Third. Onesiphorus was consistent

Again, imagine the door of Paul's prison being flung open and the guard comes in: ''Ere', you got a visitor, all the way from Ephesus he's come'—that was about 750 miles as the vulture flew, though Onesiphorus did not fly. And if the guard had added, 'Guess who it is?', I think Paul would have guessed right. Onesiphorus had already helped Paul before: 'You know very well in how many ways he helped me in Ephesus.' The phrase, 'You know very well' implies that his help was proverbial, everybody talked about it. Whenever the name of Onesiphorus came up it was always in the context of something good and encouraging. We do not know how he helped the apostle Paul in Ephesus because Paul doesn't tell us, but we are told how much it was and we are told that everybody knew about it. Not that he boasted, but that they observed. By definition you cannot hide encouragement.

Whatever Onesiphorus was in Ephesus, he was in Rome also. He could be relied upon to be the same whether in relative security or in the heat of persecution. Onesiphorus is not mentioned in the record of events in Ephesus in Acts 18 and 19, but he was clearly a significant player even then. That was seven years ago in AD 55–57, but Paul had certainly not forgotten how helpful he had been, perhaps in the time of the riot, and Timothy would know this also.

Chapter 5

When Paul offered the prayer in the first part of verse 18 that God would have mercy on the household of Onesiphorus, he knew very well that Onesiphorus would find mercy at the day of Christ when he returns in glory. Whether all his household were believers or not I do not know. But of this we can be certain: Paul knew that when Christ returned in glory Onesiphorus would not only get to heaven, of that there was no doubt, but he and the legions named after him down through the centuries of the Christian church would receive a thousand fold from the Saviour when they hear 'Well done, good and faithful encourager'.

Epaphras—a hard worker

'Epaphras, our dear fellow-servant, who is a faithful minister of Christ ... wrestling in prayer ... working hard ... my fellow prisoner' Colossians 1:7; 4:12–13; Philemon 23

Colosse was at one time an important and influential city as a gateway to Persia and distant India in the east. Situated in the valley of the Lycus River at the junction of the main trade routes from Sardis and Ephesus it was famous for its cloth, rich red dye and its agriculture and cold mountain streams. But by the time of the Roman occupation the road had been rerouted further down the valley and the town was overshadowed by Laodicea and Hierapolis—the economic and religious centres of the province of Asia respectively. This demise was hastened by a terrible earthquake in AD 60 that devastated the declining area. In spite of this, even in the time of the apostle Paul the population may have been as large as 50,000. Today the ancient town of Colosse is uninhabited.

According to Acts 19:10 Paul spent two years in Ephesus and during that time 'all the Jews and Greeks who lived in the province of Asia heard the word of the Lord.' That must have included Colosse, though apparently Paul himself never visited the city. However, a church was established there (Colossians 1:4 and 2:1) and many years later when the apostle was writing to Philemon, a wealthy resident of Colosse, he expressed his longing to visit the believers (Philemon 22). Both the founding of the young church back in AD 50, and its nurturing since then, were due to the hard work and prayers of a man called Epaphras (Colossians 1:7).

Epaphras is a shortened form of the name Epaphroditus, who we have already met in this book. The short form was perhaps to avoid confusing the two. That these two men are not the same is evident from the fact that Epaphroditus appears to be a native of Philippi (Philippians 2:25), whereas Epaphras 'who is one of you' hailed from Colosse (Colossians 4:12).

Chapter 6

How Epaphras was converted we are not told; perhaps he was on a trade mission to Ephesus on the Mediterranean coast, more than one hundred miles down the valley to the west, when he heard the gospel from Paul around AD 50. Colosse was a very religious city, where Zeus and the goddesses Ceres, Cybele and Diana (respectively Rhea, Demeter and Artemis to the Greeks) were each worshipped enthusiastically; so Epaphras may have been a convert from any one of their temples. Since his name implies that his parents had dedicated him to Aphrodite, the Greek goddess of love (she was Venus to the Romans), he was probably of Asian rather than Italian origin. For all of these reasons it is highly unlikely that he was part of the large Jewish population in the town which was perhaps as much as one fifth of the whole; though he could have been a Jewish proselyte.

When Paul wrote to the church from his house arrest in Rome in AD 60, he made no mention of the devastating earthquake that we know overtook the town in that year, so it is likely the Christians stood on the verge of a terrible and unexpected disaster. Whether Philemon or the others addressed in this letter survived, we cannot know; and Onesimus might have wished that Paul had delayed sending him back!

Largely to the credit of Epaphras, this was a well instructed church. However, elements of the mystic religions from the east which were exported along the old trade route were beginning to upset the Christian community. Some found the eastern 'hollow and deceptive philosophies' and 'the worship of angels' all very attractive. By the late '50s this false teaching had become a pressing problem and Epaphras decided to report to Paul in person and solicit his back up. The letter to the church at Colosse was the result of their conversations in Rome. Epaphras was certainly a man whom Paul could commend without reservation.

Epaphras laboured enthusiastically in ministry

Paul had sufficient knowledge of Epaphras to be able to commend his hard work. The phrase 'vouch for' (4:13) is a reference to a reliable witness. The way this man Epaphras threw himself into the gospel work was such that when the apostle picked up his pen and thought to himself: 'How best can I describe my appreciation for my brother Epaphras?' he chose a word that carried the idea of pain in toil. The phrase 'working hard' will do, though many Greek texts have another word here that means 'zeal' (hence the NKJV) implying that he was an enthusiast for the work of the gospel. Whatever word is right, it was a big recommendation, because the apostle did not suffer fools gladly and he certainly did not like lazy, disinterested and half-hearted people.

In his passionately hard work, Epaphras was not parochial. He worked hard in Colosse, but he also worked hard in neighbouring Laodicea and Hierapolis each of which was a half day's journey from Colosse. These two cities eclipsed Colosse in economics and religion, but there were Christian communities in each, and Epaphras clearly gave a lot of his time teaching, supporting and caring for them. His prayers, as we shall see shortly, were equally concerned for these three centres. He may have acted as a sort of 'itinerant elder', and as such was greatly appreciated by all the churches.

Paul's tribute that he is a 'dear fellow-servant' highlights his selfless commitment, because the word used is that of the slave. This precise word is used of Tychicus in 4:7 and stands distinct from the 'faithful servant (minister)' that follows. The word for slave is *doulos* and the word for servant is *diakonos*. The latter word does not mean that he was a deacon in the technical sense of holding an office bearing that title, but that all his ministry was given in the spirit and attitude of a humble servant of the churches. More than this, he was a 'faithful' servant, and that word means reliable, trustworthy. Paul had obviously gleaned all this not only by the reputation that came ahead of Epaphras, and his own long-standing knowledge of the man, but the fact that he had spent some time in Rome with Paul; their conversation and the prayers of Epaphras convinced the apostle of his deep commitment to the Christians in that cluster of Asian churches.

Even more important is the statement by Paul in 4:12 that Epaphras considered himself above all a 'servant (*doulos*, slave) of Christ Jesus'. That is why he was such a faithful and reliable man. His primary motivation was not simply the service of his fellow Christians, but his commitment as a bond slave to his Lord and Saviour. Epaphras was well aware of a fact that the Corinthians seemed slow to understand: that he was not his own, but he was bought at a price (1 Corinthians 6:19–20).

Epaphras served selflessly in ministry

When writing to Philemon, Paul added a further important commendation of this hard-working servant for the gospel. He is 'a fellow prisoner' (Philemon 23). Paul may have meant that literally. He had come to visit Paul in Rome and it is possible that at least temporarily he had been detained as an associate of this unusual jailbird. On the other hand it could be that Epaphras had so identified himself with Paul, sharing in whatever privations the apostle suffered, that Paul considered him a 'fellow prisoner'. If so, he would be a living example of the later encouragement to the Hebrew Christians: 'Remember those in prison as if you were their fellow prisoners' (Hebrews 13:3)—the word used here is not identical because it means literally 'bound with them', but the sense is the same.

Not all who were associated with Paul became prisoners for the gospel. In the same verse Mark, Aristarchus, Demas and Luke are referred to and they are only described as 'fellow-workers', so this may lend support to the view that Paul is speaking figuratively of Epaphras. Either way, he had so identified himself with the apostle Paul that whatever happened to Paul, Epaphras experienced as well.

Here then was a man of sweat and toil for Christ, a man of urgent perseverance. The New Testament teaches that there is only one true way of serving Christ and that is to shoulder our cross and follow him. Clearly Epaphras had done that. If our work does not cost anything, then it is probably not worth anything either.

Epaphras taught faithfully in ministry

Epaphras preached a full gospel and in such a way that the Colossians had heard, understood and responded to the truth. All this is revealed in Colossians 1:7–8. There is a slight variation here in the available manuscripts between 'on *our* behalf' and 'on *your* behalf'; was Epaphras a representative of Paul to the Colossians or of the Colossians to Paul? The balance of evidence tips in favour of 'your'. This would mean that Epaphras was a perfect representative of how the church at Colosse felt towards Paul; they could not have chosen a better man to stand in for them. On the other hand, if it refers to Epaphras as a faithful representative of

Paul, it would refer to the fact that after his conversion, presumably in Ephesus back in AD 50, he learnt the gospel so fully from Paul, and shared it so accurately with the Colossians, that Paul had every confidence that what the infant church on the banks of the River Lycus heard, was authentic Christianity.

As a result of this faithful presentation of the gospel, the people 'understood God's grace in all its truth.' Of course a true understanding of the gospel is not simply the result of a human explanation of it but of God's Holy Spirit enlightening the mind. However, because it is the work of God, that does not mean that we can put it together in any form we like or that we can be as clumsy and careless as we want and still God will speak to the sinner. He may, but that does not excuse a slovenly presentation of the truth. Epaphras knew that his task was to present the truth in the clearest possible way in order to open the understanding of their minds.

The task of Epaphras was to make the gospel understandable. We do not know how he achieved this, but we do know that it was successful—a church was born as a result. No preacher or evangelist should preach today's gospel in yesterday's language or with yesterday's congregation in mind. The evidence of his success was that they not only understood the message, but they also experienced it. The word 'understood' is a strong word. It is a strengthened form of the verb 'to know' and it means more than just knowing what something is about; the word carries the idea of a thorough knowledge. The force of this word can be seen from 1 Corinthians 13:12. In the first part of the sentence Paul used the normal word when he declared 'Now I *know* in part', he knows a little of this and a little of that, but nothing perfectly. However, in the second phrase, speaking of the change when Christ returns, he concluded 'then I shall *know fully*, even as I am *fully known*'. That is the difference!

This word had particular significance at Colosse, because among the heresies in its infancy at this time—and which endangered the young church—was that known as Gnosticism. This sect played on the word for 'knowledge', which is *gnosis* in the Greek, and taught its followers to search for a hidden and secret knowledge; the Gnostic teaching often led to extravagant and immoral life styles, which is why the apostle had to warn against lax morality in 3:5–10. Paul's word is stronger and he encouraged the church by assuring them that in Christ and the gospel they have a full understanding of the truth.

These Christians at Colosse received such an accurate and careful presentation of the truth that they could understand, respond and experience it. It was the gospel of 'God's grace in all its truth'. But there is something more here. When Paul reminded them that they 'learned' the truth from Epaphras it is the verb from which the noun 'disciple' is drawn. That they were so well taught that they became disciples of the truth is evident by the fact that their 'love in the Spirit' had been rehearsed to Paul by Epaphras. A gospel that does not result in changed lifestyles, attitudes and relationships is no gospel at all. And the consistency of this careful instruction by Epaphras was evident in the fact that ever since Paul first heard of the infant church in Colosse, and that was almost ten years ago by this time, he had had good cause to thank God and pray for them (v 9).

Epaphras was not satisfied until at Colosse, Laodicea and Hierapolis he had seen a visible church of people who understood the truth, experienced the truth and were showing evidence of the truth by their discipleship. And they had a love for all the saints (verse 4). Everything about them marked them out as people transformed by Christ. In human terms, all this was the result of the hard work of Epaphras making sure that the people were well taught, well grounded, well trained and showed evidence of love for Christ. And this is one of God's little people!

Epaphras prayed earnestly in ministry

Epaphras was also a man with an exceptional prayer life. When Paul informed the Colossians: 'He is always wrestling in prayer for you' (4:12), he must have had in his mind the many occasions when the two men had prayed around the Empire together, and Paul could only describe Epaphras as 'agonizing' in prayer. For this man, prayer was not an optional extra or a spare time leftover; he was not asking for little blessings on the church at Colosse when he happened to remember it or when he felt like it. This was a man, like Paul himself, who prayed systematically, consistently, specifically and earnestly. In this respect he was a man after Paul's own heart.

The picture Paul used here was not so much that of the competitor agonising in the Olympic games, but the soldier engaged in a furious battle—at least this is how most first century inscriptions use the word that our version weakly translates as: 'wrestling'. Prayer was never a matter of competition for Paul and his associates, but a fierce encounter with the spiritual opposition. It is the same word that Paul used in his final letter to Timothy: 'I have *fought* the good fight' (2 Timothy 4:12). When Paul remembered Epaphras on his knees, it reminded him not of an athlete in training, but a warrior in combat. A related word is used of our Lord in the Garden of Gethsemane: 'Being in *anguish*, he prayed more earnestly' (Luke 22:44); it was also used by Paul who, in his encouragement to the Christians at Rome to join him in prayer, bolted two words together meaning 'fight together' (Romans 15:30 NKJV 'strive together'). It is true that this word in time came to mean more generally to assist someone as a fellow worker, but here in Colossians Paul clearly has conflict in view.

If Epaphras was serious about prayer, he was also very specific in prayer. This was doubtless a lesson he had learnt from Paul himself. The apostle almost always told the churches precisely what it was he was praying for. See for example Ephesians 1:17–19; Philippians 1:9–11; Colossians 1:9; and 1 Thessalonians 1:2–3. Paul could recall the many times Epaphras had pleaded with God that the congregation at Colosse would stand firm, become mature and enjoy full assurance. All these were under threat from the false teaching that was creeping into the church and about which Epaphras had gone to seek advice from Paul in Rome. The fact that he had enlisted the wisdom of the apostle did not mean that he abandoned his commitment to pray.

Epaphras had also learnt consistency from Paul. The 'always' of verse 12 is reflected in Paul's letter to Philippi: 'In all my prayers for all of you, I always pray …' (1:4). He would never let a time of prayer go by without bringing the Colossians before the God of the universe. But the fact that Paul comments 'who is one of you' implies not only that Paul was aware of his generic origin, but that when he prayed, it was obvious that he belonged to them; it was not his accent that betrayed him, but his heart that formed the intensity of his battle with the evil forces liable to prevail against his friends in the Lycus valley. Shakespeare knew something about prayer when he put into the mouth of Hamlet the cry: 'My words fly up, my thoughts remain below; words without thoughts never to heaven go.' But we may improve on that, for it is doubtful whether prayers that come from a cold and indifferent heart ever reach higher than the ceiling.

Epaphras lived a Christ centred ministry

Three times Paul referred to the work of Epaphras within the context of his relationship to Jesus Christ: he is 'a faithful minister of Christ' (Colossians 1:7), 'a servant of Christ Jesus' (4:12) and 'a fellow prisoner for Christ Jesus' (Philemon 23). What struck Paul above all about this man, and it would be obvious to anyone who knew him, was that although he was motivated by a strong and enthusiastic desire to serve his fellow Christians—the repetition of 'our' in 1:7 is evidence of this—above all, his passion was to serve Christ. His highest honour was not to return to Colosse and boast that he had spent some time in the service of the apostle Paul—the only concern of Epaphras was to be in the service of Christ.

A Spartan king, when advancing against his enemy, always had with him one who had been crowned in the public games of Greece. A story tells of one such competitor who was offered a large sum of money not to compete in the games. He refused and by great effort won all his entries and was crowned. Afterwards someone came to him and asked, 'Spartan, what will you get from this victory in the games?' To which he replied, 'I shall have the honour to fight foremost in the ranks of my prince'. Such a man was Epaphras. Surely one of the greatest little people for God.

Justus—courageous humility

'Jesus, who is called Justus, also sends greetings' Colossians 4:11

Of all those whose names are mentioned in dispatches in the New Testament letters, there can be few who have so little said about them than a man whose name is Jesus, but 'who is called Justus'. In more ways than one he is one of the little people of the letters of Paul. When I first considered this man there was something that really impressed me about him but I did not think that I could justify a whole chapter to say it. But then I noticed something else that changed my mind, something that seemed to put him into a category almost on his own.

To clear the way, we need to appreciate that there are three men with this name in the New Testament. In Acts 1:23 we have the names of the two men who were candidates to take the place of Judas Iscariot as an apostle: one was called Joseph Barsabbas who was 'also known as Justus'. There is another Justus in Acts 18:7; he was a Christian at Corinth who lived next door to the synagogue and with whom Paul lodged whilst he was in the city. His full name was Titius Justus. Finally there is our man in Rome. So, here are the three men: Joseph Barsabbas Justus in Jerusalem, Titius Justus in Corinth, and Jesus Justus who is with Paul in Rome. There is no reason to connect these three because they are most likely different men and that is one reason why their full names are given to us. Our man was a friend of Paul whilst the apostle was under house arrest in Rome somewhere around the year AD 62.

Jesus Justus—a man of courage

The first thing to notice about this man are his names. His first name, which is the Jewish name Jesus, was common in the first century and earlier. It is the New Testament form of the Old Testament word Joshua and literally it means 'Yahweh (the Lord) is salvation'. This, of course, is why our Lord was given the name Jesus (Matthew 1:21). The name would be less attractive among Jews towards the middle of the first century as they would not wish their children to be identified with the blasphemous deceiver who, so they taught, performed miracles by magic and who, for his evil teaching, was justly crucified as a common criminal in the time of Pontius Pilate; his body was stolen by his followers who then put around a story of the resurrection. One leader, Rabbi Meir, would later refer to the gospel (*evangelion*) as *avengillayon*, a pun meaning 'revelation of sin'. The second name, Justus, is from the Latin which simply means just, fair or righteous.

Clearly then, Justus was his 'nickname', just as the other two men with the same name had their own names; elsewhere we have James the little, Judas Iscariot, James and John Boanerges and Joseph Barnabas. As a matter of fact the occurrence of Justus in Acts 1:23 is the only known use of this name in first century Palestine, but elsewhere there are literally hundreds of examples, especially in Rome. Outside Palestine therefore, Justus was a very common name.

The second thing that must be obvious about him is that he was a Jew. If we did not guess this from his name, it is clearly stated by Paul in verse 11. The apostle considered him also not only a Jew but a 'fellow-worker'—a word that we have already discovered in the life of Epaphroditus. In addition, he was a 'comfort'—the word of soothing that, as we have seen, had a particular significance when linked with John Mark. Beyond that we have little more information. He had two names, he was a Jew, he was a fellow-worker with Paul and he was an encouragement to the apostle.

Nevertheless, there is something outstanding about this man Jesus Justus. It is not the first thing that we may notice about him, but when we do, it simply puts everything into place and makes him all the more intriguing. Remember where Paul is. He is in Rome around the year AD 62, and he is under house arrest. There are many Christians coming and going from his house, but there are few who are prepared to take their stand by him, and what is particularly noticeable—so noticeable that Paul specifically draws attention to it—is that among those at Rome who would be classified as fellow-workers for the Kingdom of God only three were fellow Jews: Aristarchus, John Mark and Jesus who is called Justus.

That brings us directly to the courage of this man called Jesus Justus. Why were there so few Jews who supported Paul? After all, many had been converted and many of them were scattered across the Empire. There were others of course, even in Rome, who supported the apostle, but not too many that he would call fellow-workers, ready to hazard their lives and give all for the work of the gospel. Only three among his fellow countrymen, his fellow Jews, were standing by him at this time. Why does Jesus called Justus stand out, with Aristarchus and John Mark, as the three Jews who stood by Paul? The history of the answer to that question goes back some fifteen years when two events took place that bore no relationship to each other and yet clearly influenced the reason why Paul had such a high regard for Justus.

In AD 41 Tiberius Claudius Drusus Caesar became Emperor. Claudius was in many respects a most unlikely candidate, and even his sister mourned that Rome should have such an inferior Caesar. Although he was grandson to Augustus and Livia, he was weak in health and never a great military general. His only military expedition—to Britain as it happened—was to a people ready to submit virtually without a fight, and in his triumphal procession he was able to boast that he had conquered Britannia as far north as the River Thames! The Roman historian, Suetonius, tell us that he suffered from a stammer, head twitching and violent fits of rage, and that he was lazy, a gambler and ate and drank to excess. In addition he was cruel and sadistic and enjoyed both torture and executions being carried out in his presence. Many of his judicial decisions in the tribune were bizarre to the point of being comical, and for a long time he was the butt of everyone's jokes. Appropriately Nero—'the mad butcher of Rome'—was his son in law and successor. His only virtue was that he was no mean scholar and wrote books on history!

Claudius is mentioned here for one reason in particular: Suetonius tells us that 'He banished from Rome all the Jews, who were continually making disturbances at the instigation of one Chrestus'. And with this Luke agrees, recording in Acts 18:2 'Claudius had ordered all the Jews to leave Rome.' It is almost certain that the 'Chrestus' referred to by Suetonius is Christ, and the constant complaints and threats of rebellion by the Jews in various parts of the Empire over the evangelism by the Christians was sufficient for Claudius to expel all Jews from the capital.

This, of course, might explain why there were so few Jews who stood by Paul during his trial in Rome. Nero had come to power on the death of Claudius in AD 54, but there is no record of a decree allowing Jews back to

Rome and they only slowly filtered back to the city with the new regime change. However, eight years after their expulsion, not many Jewish Christians had the courage to show their face in the great metropolis. Three converted Jews stood out for their courage in doing so, and one of those was Jesus Justus.

The other and more significant event was that around the same time as the edict of Claudius, a council was held in Jerusalem by the apostles and the Christian workers to discuss a major issue. What was at stake on that occasion some fifteen years earlier was nothing less than the Christian gospel itself. There was a strong and influential party of converted Jews who agreed to salvation through Christ and the cross, but insisted upon observance of the Jewish law in order to complete the process. Their message was very simple: We are extremely happy for as many non-Jews as God calls to come and accept our Saviour but in addition they must observe certain of the Jewish ceremonies. As a result, a meeting was convened in Jerusalem, somewhere around the year AD 48, to discuss this issue. Just before the council met, I believe the apostle Paul wrote the letter to the Galatians. He wrote it for two particular reasons.

First, the churches in Galatia had been listening to the people who were teaching that non-Jews could become Christians through faith in Christ so long as they obeyed the Old Testament. So Paul wrote to correct the Galatians. But I believe he wrote it for another reason. It was just before the council of Jerusalem and Paul would be going up with Barnabas to sort this problem out once and for all. So Paul wrote a letter to the church at Galatia to head off the opposition. The tragedy was that just before this meeting in Jerusalem, the apostle learned that Peter and even Barnabas were beginning to embrace this false teaching and Peter had begun to withdraw fellowship from the Gentile converts. So, when Peter came to Antioch, perhaps on his way to Jerusalem, Paul opposed him to his face (Galatians 2:11). At the Jerusalem meeting, Paul won his case when wise old James the elder swayed the council to the truth (Acts 15:13–19). All this is very relevant for our man Justus.

In the minds of some of the converted Jews, Paul was never forgiven for the stand he took that effectively rubbished Old Testament ceremony for the life of the Christian. In fact that is the very word Paul himself used. In Philippians 3:8 he claimed, ' I consider everything a loss compared to the surpassing greatness of knowing Christ Jesus my Lord, for whose sake I have lost all things. I consider them rubbish that I may gain Christ.' And the word 'rubbish' is the word that we would use for all that goes into our dustbin or down our sewer. When Paul arrived in Jerusalem in Acts 21 the problem was still simmering.

As soon as he arrived in Jerusalem a number of the Christians came up to Paul with a problem: You can see how many thousands of Jews have become Christians, and they are all zealous for the law. But there is a danger at that very point. They have been informed that you teach all the Jews that live among the Gentiles to turn away from Moses telling them not to circumcise their children or live according to our customs; so, what shall we do? There will be trouble when they know that you are here. Paul, you are causing problems. You see Paul, if only you would comprise just a little on this issue. Does it really matter too much if the converted Jews follow their customs, so long as they don't force them on the Gentiles?

Paul was adamant on the gospel, but relented a little on the practice and went to the temple with four men who had taken a vow; unfortunately even this proved to be a questionable decision and the riot that followed led to a sequence of events that eventually landed Paul in Rome and a martyr's death. When Paul wrote to the Colossians, the problem was still real, because at the same time as writing to the Colossians he wrote to the church at Phillippi and in Phillippians 1:15 and 17 he referred to those who were preaching Christ out of rivalry, 'to stir up trouble for me while I am in chains'. They are what Paul called 'dogs' and 'mutilators of the flesh' who were forcing the Jewish ritual of circumcision on the young converts (3:2).

At the very time Paul was writing this, there were only three Jews associated with him in Rome whom he calls 'fellow-workers'. Gentile converts were supporting him, but only three Jews. Now you can understand something of the courage and the resolution of this otherwise unknown man Jesus who was called Justus. The Jews had all been expelled from Rome some years previously by a vicious emperor, and only a few with courage were venturing back. In addition to this, the Jewish Christians treated Paul with suspicion and some rejected him, contradicting his clear, uncompromising message of faith in Christ alone for salvation. As the pressure mounted, these three friends remind us of Hananiah, Azariah and Mishael, the three loyal and courageous companions of Daniel. The comfort that Justus and his friends brought Paul was no ordinary thing. The word that Paul used is not the comforter who comes along side (the *paraclete*), the word used here came originally from a noun referring to a soothing medicine; whilst it had long since become a simple word for 'consolation' we cannot forget its origin and the significance of that to Paul. The outstanding courage of Justus was a great consolation to Paul.

Jesus Justus a man of humility

However, the most obvious fact about this man is revealed in the telling phrase 'Jesus who is called Justus'. Normally we might expect him to be referred to simply as 'Jesus Justus', like 'Titius Justus' in Acts 18:7. But the form here is quite deliberate. It appears that Paul is emphasising that his name was Jesus, but we call him Justus, and he prefers that. It is not too hard to understand why. For Christians, the name Jesus, though common in the first century, had become a very special name. Justus now decided that he could not carry the name of his own Lord and Saviour, so he requested the family name of Jesus should be dropped and he adopted the name of Justus instead.

Another man may have owned the name of Jesus with pride and even boasted of it and ransacked his genealogy to find some connection, but not this one. He was not only a courageous man but he was a very humble man as well. In spite of his courage and his loyalty to Paul and the gospel, all of which was outstanding, he is little known. In fact he is even less known than you think. If you turn to Paul's letter to Philemon, that short letter that went along with the letter to the Colossians, you will notice that Aristarchus and John Mark are both there, along with Epaphras, Luke and even Demas, but there is no mention of Jesus who is called Justus (Philemon 23–24). Some commentators say he must have been omitted by an oversight—but the Holy Spirit does not have oversights. Here is a humble man who stepped back from the limelight so much that God chose to overlook him in order to enhance his reputation for humility!

Priscilla and Aquila—at home for Christ

'After this, Paul left Athens and went to Corinth. There he met a Jew named Aquila, a native of Pontus, who had recently come from Italy with his wife Priscilla, because Claudius had ordered all the Jews to leave Rome. Paul went to see them, and because he was a tentmaker as they were, he stayed and worked with them. Every Sabbath he reasoned in the synagogue, trying to persuade Jews and Greeks' Acts 18:1–4.

In the first century, Pontus was a Roman province situated on the southern shores of the Black Sea (known then as Euxine). Nestling beneath a mountain range, the fertile plain was famous for its fruits—especially cherries, which the emperor Lusullus first brought to Europe in 72 BC. The region also traded in such diverse commodities as wine, grain, wood, honey, iron, steel and salt. There was a sizeable Jewish community in Pontus, and the gospel first came here when Jews and proselytes, converted by the powerful work of the Spirit on the day of Pentecost, returned home with the good news (Acts 2:9). Tradition claims that Andrew and Thaddeus evangelised the area.

Aquila was a Jewish leatherworker who, together with his wife Priscilla, lived in this distant part of the Roman Empire. There have been odd attempts to interpret his trade as a 'landscape painter' or 'shoemaker', but there can be no reasonable doubt that the traditional translation is correct. The verb often refers to making small tents for the use of travellers, from leather, goat's hair, cloth or linen, and in the Greek translation of the Old Testament the noun was used of the Tabernacle (for example Exodus 25:9); in the light of the constant moving of Aquila and his wife, they may well have needed the product of their own trade!

Just when and how they were converted to Christ we do not know. It is possible that they were Jewish proselytes who returned from their pilgrimage to Jerusalem having heard the message of the gospel through the preaching of Peter on the day of Pentecost. But that would have been twenty years before we meet them first in Acts 18; it is as likely that they were converted through the witness of the first generation of Christians in that area. For some reason they left their home town and took up residence in the great city of Rome.

In the story of Justus we noted that the Roman Emperor Claudius was a tragic and comical figure of fun who, surprisingly, later became a very popular emperor—for a while at least. Claudius set out to restore the ancient Roman religions, and as an early step, in the year AD 49 he expelled all the Jews from Rome. The Roman historian Suetonius records: 'He banished from Rome all the Jews, who were continually making disturbances at the instigation of one Chrestus.' Whether Chrestus is a reference to Christ, which is most likely, or simply to a Jewish insurgent, Priscilla and Aquila found themselves in Corinth, set up in business and opened their home. It was here that Paul met them. We will come to the rest of their story shortly, but already you can see that there was a boldness about the distinctive evangelistic witness of this husband and wife that gives them a rightful place as a model for every Christian family. If the cause of the expulsion of the Jews from Rome, recorded in Acts 2:9 and by Suetonius, was the new teaching about Christ, then Priscilla and Aquila were clearly at the forefront of evangelism. Christians must have been particularly unpopular among the Jews because it was their fault that all Jews were turned out of Rome in AD 49.

Corinth was an international seaport and a busy cosmopolitan centre for trade. Aquila and his wife set up their home and business, soon found a church, and quickly began to witness to their faith. When Paul arrived one year later they were already well-known. For this couple there was no question of keeping a low profile, or cooling their witness, and immediately their home was open for the gospel. Priscilla could not long have finished unpacking the boxes, and Aquila had barely re-established his business and organised his work bench when along came Paul—a man too hot for most to handle. Behind him at Philippi, Thessalonica, and Berea lay a string of riots, and trouble was brewing at Athens which he had recently left. This fiery evangelical knocked on their door and unhesitatingly they took him in—for eighteen months!

The very next Sabbath, Paul was out on the streets and in the synagogue. That was dangerous—and not least for Priscilla and Aquila. When the going became hot Paul could move on, but they lived here. Was it their courage in Corinth that led Paul to comment later to the church at Rome: 'They risked their lives for me' (Romans 16:4)? But they were equally in danger when they moved to Ephesus with Paul (Acts 18:18); in his letter written from Ephesus to the Christians at Corinth, Paul commented that he intended to stay in Ephesus until the Spring because a great door for effective work had been opened to him, and then he added ominously: 'and there are many who oppose me' (1 Corinthians 16:9). Those enemies of Paul were inevitably enemies of Aquila and Priscilla. They were undoubtedly an outstanding husband and wife team and this is why Paul could add: 'Not only I but all the churches of the Gentiles are grateful to them' (Romans 16:4). It was not only their home but their lives that were at the disposal of Christ.

To back track a little, when Paul moved on to Ephesus after eighteen months in Corinth, he was, according to Acts 18:18 'accompanied by Aquila and Priscilla'—their home and business were on the move yet again. Here at Ephesus they set up home and Paul, after a very short stay, travelled through Pisidia, Galatia and Phrygia visiting the young churches, before returning to Ephesus two years later in AD 55 settling once again, we may assume though it is not certain, with his loyal friends Aquila and Priscilla. During Paul's absence they had helped a young man named Apollos.

Aquila and Priscilla were still in Ephesus when Paul wrote his first letter to the church at Corinth from the city because he adds: 'The churches in the province of Asia send you greetings. Aquila and Priscilla greet you warmly in the Lord, and so does the church that meets in their house' (1 Corinthians 16:19). Later, possibly after the death of Claudius in AD 54 and after Paul left Ephesus in AD 57, they returned to Rome. When Paul arrived in Greece (Acts 20:2) around AD 58, he stayed for three months in Corinth and from here wrote his letter to the church at Rome in which, among many greetings sent to the members at Rome, Paul particularly mentioned Priscilla and

Aquila and 'the church that meets at their house' (Romans 16:5). Perhaps they were still there when Paul himself arrived in Rome around AD 62, but according to his correspondence with Timothy they were soon back in Ephesus: 'Greet Priscilla and Aquila and the household of Onesiphorus' (2 Timothy 4:19). Are you confused at their movements? Perhaps Priscilla was too! Like exiles or asylum seekers, this couple appeared to have no fixed home: Pontus—Rome—Corinth—Ephesus—back to Rome—and finally (?) to Ephesus again. But wherever their home was, they were always at home for Christ.

Paul refers to the wife as Prisca, which is the formal and full name, whilst Luke in his story of the early church sent to Theophilus, refers to her as Priscilla, which is the diminutive or 'pet' form (compare Elizabeth and Betty)—though this distinction is not apparent in some of our translations. Four of the six references to this couple place Priscilla first. This may imply that she was a citizen of high rank, or possibly that she was more active in the church; some have concluded that Priscilla was the more able teacher and theologian of the two, and Professor Harnack even offers her as the most likely author of the letter to the Hebrews! This is all unnecessary speculation when the more apparent reason for this order is that mere convention placed the lady's name first—just as often on the continent of Europe today.

However, one thing that is both certain and unique about this couple in the New Testament records, is that although they are referred to on six different occasions in four different Bible books, they are never referred to without the name of their partner added. It is always 'Priscilla and Aquila' or 'Aquila and Priscilla' but never the one without the other. That must surely tell us that in the mind of the early church, and Paul in particular, these two were always considered, in today's language, 'an item'. They worked so much as a team—whether offering warm Christian hospitality or carefully explaining the Christian faith to a young convert—that you could never think of the one without the other. There can surely be no greater tribute to a husband and wife than that.

However, what for us is most significant, is that of the six references to them, four refer directly to their home and one by implication. Only the final greeting from Paul via Timothy makes no reference to their hospitality. That, therefore will be our focus. How did Priscilla and Aquila use their home?

Their home was a guest house

Paul had experienced the open home of this couple, and when in Romans 12:13 he wrote of the spiritual gift of hospitality, doubtless he had Priscilla and Aquila in mind. In the New Testament the word 'hospitality' literally means 'a love for strangers'. Hospitality is not entertaining our friends and family, but opening our homes to those we do not know. Our Lord has some very clear and decisive things to say about hospitality and it is recorded in Luke 14:12–13, 'Then Jesus said to his host, "When you give a luncheon or dinner, do not invite your friends, your brothers or relatives, or your rich neighbours; if you do, they may invite you back and so you will be repaid. But when you give a banquet, invite the poor, the crippled, the lame, the blind, and you will be blessed. Although they cannot repay you, you will be repaid at the resurrection of the righteous."' Those are uncomfortable words.

Of course, this is not to deny the importance of hospitality to the Lord's people. Paul encouraged the Christians at Rome to welcome Phoebe 'in a way worthy of the saints' (Romans 16:2). For his part, Peter 'rubbed in' his Master's teaching when he urged the churches: 'Offer hospitality to one another without grumbling' (1 Peter 4:9). The phrase 'to one another' is not limited simply to our friends in the local church. Peter's letter was addressed to: 'God's elect, strangers in the world, scattered throughout Pontus [note that especially], Galatia, Cappadocia, Asia and Bithynia'; in other words this was an encouragement for an open home for Christian strangers; a fact that is impressed plainly by Hebrews 13:2, 'Do not forget to entertain strangers, for by so doing some people have entertained angels without knowing it.' The Christian home should never be a castle or a palace, but a guest house. Hospitality is an immense privilege, and the apostle Paul—no less—signed the guestbook in the home of this couple.

I love people staying in my home, and my late wife, Barbara, was a superb hostess for the many who stayed with us for longer or shorter periods and she prepared hundreds of meals over the years. However, among the many occupations that I would not choose would be that of running a regular guest house! It is clearly very hard work. When Paul referred to Priscilla and Aquila as 'fellow-workers' (Romans 16:3), it is one of those occasions when he placed Priscilla first; that was perhaps significant. Who cooked the meals and made up the bed? Who fussed over Paul when he returned weary from a long day debating or bruised after being roughed-up by hecklers? A modern generation may scoff at the quaint notion of the lady of the house working hard to make sure her guests were comfortable and well fed—but neither Paul nor his Master mocked at such a vital ministry. Mark specifically referred to Mary Magdalene, Mary the mother of James the younger and of Joses, and Salome, who in Galilee: 'had followed [Jesus] and cared for his needs' (Mark 15:40–41). And in his long list of personal greetings in Romans 16 Paul referred to the mother of Rufus (had he forgotten her name?) 'who has been a mother to me' (v 13). What fellow-workers these all were.

We have met this phrase 'fellow-worker' before among the little people of the New Testament. Besides this reference here, Paul used it no less than eight times in his letters, referring to Urbanus, Timothy, Titus, Epaphroditus, Peter, Apollos, Justus, Aristarcus, John Mark, Clement— and even Euodia and Syntyche! There are a thousand ways to serve the Lord, and the open guest house of this warm-hearted couple was no less service than the foot-slogging Tychicus who travelled the churches troubleshooting for Paul.

Their home was a teaching centre

Priscilla and Aquila arrived ahead of Paul in Ephesus, and here their attention was drawn to a young evangelist who began to preach in the synagogue. They listened and soon discovered that his zeal was undoubted, his gift of preaching and persuading was equally undoubted, but something was not quite right with his theology: 'A Jew named Apollos, a native of Alexandria, came to Ephesus. He was a learned man, with a thorough knowledge of the Scriptures. He had been instructed in the way of the Lord, and he spoke with great fervour and talked about Jesus accurately, though he knew only the baptism of John. He began to speak boldly in the synagogue. When Priscilla and Aquila heard him, they invited him into their home and explained to him the way of God more adequately.

When Apollos wanted to go to Achaia, the brothers encouraged him and wrote to the disciples there to welcome him. On arriving, he was a great help to those who by grace had believed. For he vigorously refuted the Jews in public debate, proving from the Scriptures that Jesus was the Christ' (Acts 18:24–28).

Apollos, or to give him his full name, Apollonius, came from Alexandria, the administrative capital of Roman Egypt and an important banking and trading centre. Above all, however, it was a renowned seat of learning with a university and library that filled much of the Empire with envy; only Athens and Jerusalem could vie with it for scholarship. Even the large Jewish community in the city represented the intellectual elite of the Jewish world. Here the Greek translation of the Old Testament (the Septuagint) had been produced three hundred years earlier, and study of the Scriptures was vigorously pursued by the learned rabbis, giving rise to a new and energetic interpretation of the Hebrew sacred writings.

From the fact that Apollos was 'a learned man, with a thorough knowledge of the Scriptures' (v 24), it is evident that he had enjoyed the best possible education and came to faith in Christ as one of the bright young graduates of his day. The word 'learned' has two meanings in Greek literature of the time: it can refer to someone who is well educated in literature, the arts and history—a man of letters—or it may refer to someone with the gift of reasoned debate or a skilled orator (hence many translations have 'eloquent'). In view of the commendation of his debating powers in the following verse: 'he spoke with great fervour and taught about Jesus accurately' it is more likely that the word 'learned' refers to his sharp mind and good education. Whatever the precise meaning, as Aquila and Priscilla listened to his preaching, they knew that something was missing. So they immediately invited Apollos into their home.

What was wrong with the teaching of Apollos was that he 'knew only the baptism of John' (Acts 18:25). Clearly there were a number of Christians in Ephesus who were equally deficient, in fact some may well have been the product of the incomplete teaching of Apollos. When Paul arrived in the city he discovered twelve men who, though truly converted, knew nothing about the Holy Spirit. It is always possible for a young Christian to be ignorant of the great Christian truths that they have in reality experienced.

What interests us here is not the inadequacy of Apollos, but the reaction of Aquila. He and his wife did not waylay him in the street, harangue him in the synagogue, or pillory him in the congregation. They invited him into their home.

In the privacy of their own home, Priscilla and Aquila filled in the gaps of his theology. Aquila was acting as a true elder: 'able to teach' (1 Timothy 3:2), and between them they were 'hospitable' (Titus 1:8). The future success of Apollos as a preacher and debater when he moved on to Corinth (Acts 18:27–28) was more due to the careful tuition in the seclusion of the home of Aquila than to the learned professors at Alexandria. His skilful eloquence that drew a factious party around him in Corinth (1 Corinthians 1:12) was not his fault. We should never underestimate the long-term value of personal tuition by an older and wiser Christian. Every young Christian needs a mentor.

Instruction is not an intrusion. In the security of our Christian homes there should be discussion between family, friends and strangers on a whole range of Christian issues from theology to our personal experience. We can all talk about a thousand subjects from politics to parenting, from sport to education and from holidays to home decorating, but it should all be in the context of our Christian faith. Many older Christians would consider it an impertinence to support a younger Christian by gently correcting his errors in belief or practice. But what did Paul mean when he encouraged the older women to: 'train the younger women to love their husbands and children, to be self controlled and pure, to be busy at home, to be kind and to be subject to their husbands, so that no one will malign the word of God' (Titus 2:3–5)? And what better place than in the home? And are younger women and younger men too proud and too self-assured to take advice from older and more experienced Christians? Apollos clearly was not reluctant to receive this home instruction, and Aquila and Priscilla were not afraid to give it either.

What is more, they did not simply tell Apollos to 'wait until Paul arrives and he will sort you out'. Why is the pastor always the first line of defence against error and half truths? In our churches there should be an army of wise older Christians who can 'teach others also'. Significantly, this couple who hailed from a far distant outpost of the empire and boasted nothing more than their trade of tent making, were not intimidated by the educational prowess of this young graduate from the highest hall of learning that the Empire could offer. Clever he may be, well versed in the Old Testament Scriptures also, sharp and decisive in argument and debate he clearly was, but what mattered above all was that he should have a firm grasp of the faith once and for all delivered to the saints. Aquila and Priscilla knew that and, fortunately for the church at Ephesus and the community at large, so did Apollos.

Their home was a house church

Writing to the Christians in the city of Rome, Paul sent greetings to Priscilla and Aquila and 'the church that meets at their house' (Romans 16:5); similarly, from Ephesus this couple sent greetings to the church at Corinth: 'and so does the church that meets at their house' (1 Corinthians 16:19). Since both in Rome and in Corinth the community of Christians gathered in their home, we may presume that Aquila ran a successful business and they were able to afford a modestly large home; certainly they had no problem in accommodating Paul during his eighteen month stay in Corinth.

But to open their home for the regular Christian meetings, was a risky business. In this home people talked of Jesus Christ and prayed to him; it would soon be known where the Christians were meeting, and with the background of riots Paul so often unintentionally left as a legacy in the towns he visited, this was considerably dangerous. But aside from the danger, here was a home where the husband and wife prayed and read the Scriptures regularly and, if they had children and servants, no doubt they were part of the family worship also. Equally, when relations or visitors called by, they would experience a home saturated in Christian conversation and worship—not all the time, but at any time. We cannot imagine that this was a home of grumbling, complaining and criticising; here people came and went freely, and they were lifted and encouraged. It was good to be in their home, you could experience a little of heaven when you shared the table with Aquila and Priscilla.

Centuries before, when Job experienced the loss of everything that was most dear to him: his reputation, friends, and personal health, what pained him more than anything was his remembrance of the precious times he had spent with his family. Job looked back to the days: 'When God's intimate friendship blessed my house, when the Almighty was still with me and my children were around me, when my path was drenched with cream and the rock poured out for me streams of olive oil' (Job 29:4–6).

There may be legal and logistical reasons why generally speaking we no longer meet in individual homes for our regular church gatherings. However it would be a tragedy if in any one of our homes it could be said that no Christian (friend or stranger) ever entered, that the worship of God never took place corporately, and the conversation rarely turned to issues above and beyond the mundane world of work, finance, sport or politics. Sadly, many teenagers from Christian homes know nothing of family prayers and have no example of discussing Christian matters beyond the regular complaining about the members or leaders of the church.

Because this subject is so vital for our churches today, I will close with three small cameos of Christian homes. The first was written by Tertullian, a Christian leader in North Africa in the second century: 'What a blessed thing is the marriage of true believers, of one hope, one discipline, servants of the same Master! ... Together they offer up their prayers—together they lie in the dust, and keep their fasts, teaching each other, exhorting each other, bearing up each other. They are together in God's church, together in God's peace, together in straits, persecutions, consolations; freely the sick are visited and the poor supported; there are alms without trouble; sacrifices without scruple; daily unimpeded diligence. Christ sees it and rejoices.'

The second is from the pen of Jonathan Edwards, the eighteenth century New England pastor: 'Every Christian family ought to be as it were a little church, consecrated to Christ, and wholly influenced and governed by his rules. And family education and order are some of the chief of the means of grace.'

Finally, when George Whitefield, the great evangelist and preacher from England stayed in the home of Jonathan Edwards he wrote in his journal for Sunday 19 October 1740: 'Felt great satisfaction in being at the house of Mr Edwards. A sweeter couple I have not yet seen. Their children were not dressed in silks and satins, but plain, as become the children of those who, in all things, ought to be examples of Christian simplicity. Susannah Edwards is adorned with a meek and quiet spirit; she talked solidly of the things of God, and seemed to be such a helpmeet for her husband, that she caused me to renew those prayers, which, for some months, I have put up to God, that he would be pleased to send me a daughter of Abraham to be my wife.' The influence of the Edwards home was significant—two years later George married Elizabeth James!

Every Christian family should strive to be an example of hospitality, Christian instruction and devoted worship to Christ—and the best template we have is the home of Aquila and Priscilla.

A gathering of God's little people—in the church at Rome

'Everyone has heard about your obedience, so I am full of joy over you' Romans 16:19

When Paul wrote to the church at Rome and invited them to 'join me in my struggle' (15:30), he was writing to a church that he had never visited, although clearly he knew many of the Christians there. He was writing around AD 57 on his third visit to Corinth in Greece. During his first visit to the city, the synagogue ruler, Crispus, had been converted and, according to 1 Corinthians 1:14, both he and Gaius were baptised by Paul. Romans 16:23, implies that not only did the church at Rome meet in the home of Gaius, but that Paul himself was staying there. Wherever Paul travelled, he discovered the privilege of belonging to the Christian community which was made up of ordinary men and women whose Christian love, hard work, and faithful, courageous witness was the heartbeat and backbone of the gospel work. We often think only of Paul encircling the Roman Empire with the message of Christ, but without an army of God's little people, he would have achieved nothing—and he knew this. When the apostle invited some of God's little people to join him in the struggle, he knew the quality of these Christian legionnaires.

Precisely who founded the church in Rome we do not know; it was hardly likely to have been Peter, who does not even get a mention in Romans 16! Perhaps it was Aquila and Priscilla, who may have been converted at Pentecost some thirty years earlier. But it is equally likely that the church was started by an unnamed Christian returning after Pentecost and sharing the good news with his or her neighbours. Some of the greatest gospel work has been accomplished by believers whose names have never come down to us.

On Sunday morning, 6th January 1850, Charles Haddon Spurgeon was a miserable teenager who turned into Artillery Street Methodist Chapel in Newmarket; it was a foul day of heavy wind and snow. An old man was preaching in the place of the appointed preacher. He preached a passionate, but hardly eloquent sermon, from Isaiah 45:22. Spurgeon, who was to become the 'Prince of Preachers', fill the Metropolitan Tabernacle with over six thousand people every Sunday evening and who is still widely read today, was converted in a moment. Many years later, at least three people claimed the honour to have been preaching on that occasion, but Spurgeon recognised none of them! The man who finally led Charles Haddon Spurgeon to Christ remains unknown on earth to this day.

Whilst Paul commonly closed his letters with greetings from those with him at the time of writing and to some of those in the church he is addressing, his letter to the church at Rome is unusual in the fulness of the list.

Those who received greetings

There are many legends and even more speculations identifying the names in this list, and we must tread cautiously to avoid both. A little detective work and reasonable assumption is wiser than wild speculation.

Phoebe (vs 1–2) was very likely the one who carried the letter from Corinth to Rome, perhaps in the course of her business trips, but so much has been said about her and claimed for her that we must return to her in a later study of *God's little women in the Bible*, which is the third book in this series.

Two couples are mentioned by Paul: The first are **Priscilla and Aquila** (vs 3–5) who we have described in the previous chapter; wherever they settled, they were such an asset to the church that 'all the churches of the Gentiles are grateful to them.' They were Jewish converts, and therefore their open heart and home were all the more appreciated by the Gentile churches; it is very unlikely that *they* had been caught up in the false gospel that had been spread around by ex-Jews insistent on turning every young convert from the Gentile world into a law-observing Jew, and which had caused so much agony and division in the early days of the Gospel. This couple, using their home as a guest house, teaching centre and house church were 'risk-takers' for the gospel. But we need say no more about them here, except that they may have been Paul's source of so much of his information about the members at Rome; they had left Rome and headed for Corinth some eight years earlier when the Emperor Claudius threw all Jews out of the capital.

Andronicus and Junias (v 7) were possibly another husband and wife team. I say 'possibly' because it is uncertain whether Junias is male or female, and whether they may have been father and son or two brothers. The name Andronicus appears in the list of Caesar's servants, but we cannot make a certain connection. There would be nothing unusual about this, since in this very chapter the 'city director of public works' at Corinth added his greetings to the closing part of the letter (v 23).

We are told four things about this encouraging pair.

They are 'relatives' of Paul. The word literally means 'kinsmen' and can equally be translated as blood relatives or fellow countrymen; if the latter, Paul is referring to the fact that they are fellow Jews. The same word is used of **Herodion** (v 11) and of Lucius, Jason and Sosipater (v 21), and this is the way Paul used it in Romans 9:3. However, Aquila and Priscilla were also Jews, and the word is not used to describe them. If they are blood relatives, it is thrilling to see how many of Paul's family had become Christians.

What is more important to notice is that they had 'been in prison with me' (v 7). That phrase translates just two words in the Greek: 'my *fellow-prisoners*' (where *fellow-prisoners* is one word), and it is the exact expression that is used to refer to Aristarchus (Colossians 4:10) and Epaphras (Philemon 23). We are not told that Paul had been in prison in Corinth, so we are left to guess just what prison cell they shared with Paul and why, though clearly the church at Rome knew all about it. The phrase could possibly refer to the fact that they regularly visited Paul in prison, though no one visited more regularly than Onesiphorus and he is not described in this way. However, if they did share his imprisonment, even voluntarily by spending so much time with him and regularly providing for his needs, then, as we commented on Epaphras, they were living examples of Hebrews 13:3 'Remember those in prison as if you were their *fellow-prisoners*' (here the word is not identical but means 'bound together with them'). Whether prisoners literally or pastorally, Andronicus and Junias were real soldiers of the cross.

When Paul commented that they were 'outstanding among the apostles' (v 7), he little realised the debate that simple expression would cause two millenniums later! Is it to be read that they were outstanding 'as apostles', and would this therefore be evidence that the line of apostolic authority did not end with the Twelve plus Paul; and that it was not confined to men either? Or is it a more loose use of the word 'apostle' which simply refers to 'a messenger'? Or is it to be read that they had an outstanding reputation 'among the (thirteen) apostles'? The latter is so much to be preferred, if only because it is the more natural sense, and to take it any other way would mean that it stands alone in the New Testament supporting a continuing, and female, line of apostles. Their reputation among the apostles was significant: the word refers to something of note and comes from a root meaning a sign; it can refer to something either notorious or illustrious! 'Outstanding' (NIV) may be a little extravagant, whilst 'well-known' (*English Standard Version*) is perhaps a little weak; the *Authorised Version* 'of note' is at least accurate but hardly tells us whether this was for good or bad. However, to have such a reputation among the apostles that they all thought well of them and noted the good work that they had so unselfishly done, was high praise indeed. It is always encouraging when God's little people are both noted and praised for the work that they do in serving the church. One mark of Paul's clear leadership qualities was his regular expression of appreciation and congratulation. A tradition tells us that this couple founded the church at Rome—perhaps that is better than the tradition that Peter did, but who knows?

Finally, we are told that Andronicus and Junias were 'in Christ before I was'. That is much more significant than may at first appear. By this time, Paul himself had been a Christian for some twenty-five years, so these two were not exactly in the spring time of life when the average age span across the Roman Empire could hardly have been more than forty at best. In the early church, seniority was respected—and so it should be today. Paul encouraged Titus: 'Likewise, teach the older women to be reverent in the way they live, not to be slanderers or addicted to much wine, but to teach what is good. Then they can train the younger women ...' (Titus 2:3–4), and Peter urged 'Young men ... be submissive to those who are older' (1 Peter 5:5). Paul respected this older couple who refused to allow their advancing age to disqualify them from the honour and value of Christian service. Old age need never hinder our service in prayer, which is at the coalface of Christian work. If these 'relatives' of Paul were 'in Christ' some time before he himself was converted so dramatically on the road to Damascus, could it be that hidden behind this simple statement is Paul's knowledge that they had long been praying for their vicious kinsman who was a ruthless enemy of the gospel and of all who followed 'the way'? I have often noticed that when someone comes to faith in Christ, we soon discover those who had been praying for them for so long.

Epenetus (v 5) was 'the first convert to Christ in the province of Asia'—not 'Achaia' (Greece) as some translations read, because according to 1 Corinthians 16:15 the household of Stephanas were the first converts in Achaia. He was a 'dear friend' of Paul and, like Andronicus and Junias, he must have been one of the more senior members of the church at Rome. Unless the phrase means that he was the first of Paul's converts in Asia, Epenetus must have been converted at Pentecost since we know that residents from Asia were present then (Acts 2:9).

The first record of Paul reaching the Roman province of Asia is when he preached at Ephesus (Acts 19:1). Perhaps this was the birth place of Epenetus and the occasion of his new birth. His name means 'praiseworthy'—and indeed he was. Our translators have missed the emphasis of Paul here, because what he actually wrote was: 'The *first-fruit* of Asia *for* Christ'. Of course this means the first convert, but the 'first-fruit' was a word familiar to all Jews as an expression of great joy in the beginning of an abundant harvest that would be dedicated to God (Exodus 23:19), and Paul himself had already used it to refer to the gift of the Holy Spirit being the promise of much more to come (Romans 8:23).

There was probably never such joy among the early Baptist missionaries to India than they experienced at the baptism in the River Ganges of the Hindu teacher Krishna Pal on Sunday 28 December 1800. William Carey and his team believed that 'a continent was coming behind him'; he was the first-fruit of their seven years of labour in India. Paul felt the same about Epenetus.

Mary (v 6) is one of six women in the New Testament with this very common name, but she made an uncommon contribution to gospel work. Her very hard work for the church was well known among the Christians at

Rome, and perhaps it provides a neat balance to the sister of Martha who was commended not for her work but for her worship (Luke 10:41–42). Notice that Paul commented that Mary worked 'for' the church at Rome; there is a real servanthood here as she gave herself 'for' the believers—and this neat distinction was not lost on Paul. However, her hard work was not unique. **Tryphena and Tryphosa** (v 12) were equally hard working despite their names, which are both derived from 'luxury' and mean 'delicate' and 'dainty'! Several examples of these names appear in Caesar's household during Paul's time but we have no evidence that was *their* occupation. Almost certainly they were sisters, and from their similar names it would be reasonable to assume that they were twins. They provide a refreshing contrast to Syntyche and Euodia (Philippians 4:2) whose relationship stank in the church—in spite of Euodia's beautiful name which means fragrant! They too had been hardworking, though much of their good was undone by petty and catty quarrelling. Tryphena and Tryphosa appear to have been a united pair of sisters in every sense of that word 'sisters', because their hard work was evidently 'in the Lord'.

Persis (v 12) was another woman who worked hard 'in the Lord' and she is described simply as '*the* dear Persis' (the NIV is incorrect here), which is to be contrasted to 'my dear Stachys' in v 9; his is a personal endearment, whilst hers reflects what everyone thinks of her. It may be significant that Paul refers to two men (Epenetus and Stachys) as '*my* dear' and to Persis as '*the* dear'; perhaps it was a deliberately cautious and modest way of referring to one who may have been a young lady in the church. On the other hand, the past tense 'has worked' could imply that age or ill health now hindered Persis from her previous work—but past faithfulness will not be overlooked by Paul.

In this final chapter of Paul's letter to Rome, the phrases 'in Christ' and 'in the Lord' occur eleven times. What is its significance? Paul described the Christian in this way: 'If anyone is in Christ, he is a new creation …' (2 Corinthians 5:17). It can mean that we are 'in the good of'; that is, all the benefits from Christ (forgiveness, reconciliation, promises etc.) are ours. Or, it can mean 'in the cause of'; in other words, we are associated with him in the gospel work. But above all, it must refer to the spiritual union of the believer with Christ and thus with each other. When Jesus prayed for his disciples 'that all of them may be one, just as you, Father, are in me and I am in you. May they also be in us ...' (John 17:21) he was referring to the spiritual union of Christ with his Father, of his people with him, and of them with each other. The hard work of Persis and others should be an outcome of the spiritual unity and fellowship that we enjoy by being part of the church and united to Christ.

Ampliatus (v 8) was dearly loved by Paul; his name, incidentally, also appears in the Imperial household, and on a first century tomb, but neither need be our man; it was a common name at the time, especially among slaves. On the other hand, we know that Christians were already working close to the emperor because in Philippians 4:22 Paul rounded off his letter with his usual cluster of greetings 'especially those who belong to Caesar's household.' **Urbanus** (v 9) was another 'fellow-worker', **Stachys** was a 'dear friend', and **Apelles** (v 10) was 'tested and approved'. Our translators are here trying to convey the meaning of one simple word *dokimos*. At this time there was no paper money, and all coinage was made from metal, not infrequently silver. When first minted, the coins were rough and needed to be smoothed off round the edges; unscrupulous merchants would shave off more than necessary to gain extra metal. At one point, more than eighty laws were passed in Athens to stop the practice of shaving down the coins then in circulation. An honest merchant would neither shave coins nor accept coins that had been tampered with; it was considered counterfeit. Men of integrity like this were called *dokimos* or 'approved'. The cheats were *adokimos*, and this word is variously translated in Paul's letters by 'disqualified' (1 Corinthians 9:27), 'failed' (2 Corinthians 13:6), 'rejected' (2 Timothy 3:8) and 'unfit' (Titus 1:16). Apelles has been tested and approved, not as a counterfeit, but as a gospel merchant of the highest integrity.

An **Aristobulus** (v 10) was a grandson of Herod the Great, but that only proves the name was common in the first century and reminds us that these were dangerous days to be a Christian. The words 'belong to the household' (and 'in the household' v 11) are not in Paul's letter but have been added by the translators in an attempt to make sense. Either it refers to the family, or more likely, the household of servants and slaves; Aristobulus and **Narcissus** may not be believers at all, but owners of a large and wealthy estate. There may be something sadly significant in the way Paul addressed Narcissus (v 11), not so much that the name refers to a young man in Greek mythology and a flower that was used to produce a narcotic, but that Paul referred pointedly to 'those (in the household) of Narcissus who are in the Lord'—clearly all were not.

Why **Rufus** should be singled out as 'chosen in the Lord' (v 13) when, in fact, they all were, is not easy to discern; unless there is a hint, taken up in very early traditions, that he is the brother of Alexander, whose father, Simon, carried the cross of our Lord to Golgotha (Mark 15:21). However, I suspect it is actually his mother that Paul had particularly in mind. Literally, Paul referred to 'his mother and mine'. The NIV has paraphrased it, perhaps not unjustly, as 'who has been a mother to me, too.' In what ways she had mothered Paul in his times of need, we just do not know. Was it baked cakes, dressing wounds, mending torn clothes and replacing worn ones? Paul knew, and her Saviour knew, and that is surely all that mattered to the mother of Rufus. We do not even know her name—surely Paul had not forgotten it. But there are so many like her in the church, and always have been. The world mocks and scorns such little jobs by these little women, but the Master praises and so did Paul.

Just who '**Asyncritus, Phlegon, Hermes, Patrobas, Hermas** and the brothers with them' (v 14) were, we can have little idea; perhaps they were slaves? Nor have we any better handle on **Philologus, Julia, Nereus** and **Olympas**, except that Paul seemed to have forgotten the name of the sister of Nereus!

Those who sent greetings

It was usual for Paul to sign off a letter himself (see 2 Thessalonians 3:17) even when, as seems to be mostly the case, he used a friend to take down his dictation. Often those around him at the point when the letter came to an end, would be eager to send their greetings to known and unknown friends. Clearly there was a lot of movement among the churches in the first century, with Christians visiting on business and even for family visits. A number of those mentioned in this chapter had obviously worked with Paul elsewhere. With the danger of false apostles and those pretending to speak or write in the name of Paul, letters of introduction became a necessary and regular part of church life (1 Corinthians 16:3 and 2 Corinthians 3:1). **Tertius** wrote this letter for Paul (v 22) and added his own personal word of greetings 'I, Tertius … greet you in the Lord.'

Timothy is, of course well known, and would shortly be settled at Ephesus where Paul would send him two letters of encouragement and instruction. Of **Lucius** we know nothing except that there is another Lucius in Acts 13:1, but it is impossible to make a connection. **Jason** bears a name that we may link to the host of Paul and Silas in Thessalonica (Acts 17:5–9); poor Jason found himself caught up in a riot and was roughly dragged before the city officials before released on bail. We meet a **Sosipater** in Acts 20:4 ('Sopater' is the same name) at Berea, and we know that his father was one Pyrrhus. He later accompanied Paul to Asia and this could be the same man. If so, these two men, Jason and Sosipater, are linked because they are both converted Jews who hailed from Macedonia.

Of **Gaius** (v 23) we have tantalising connections. There is a travelling companion of Paul from Macedonia who, together with Aristarchus, was caught up in the riot at Ephesus (Acts 19:29); this one is not likely to be the same Gaius as the one referred to in Acts 20:4 as 'from Derbe' since that city was in Lycaonia and not Macedonia. But he is very likely the same Gaius as the one Paul refers to in 1 Corinthians 1:14 as one of the few whom the apostle baptised at Corinth. Then there is the Gaius whom John addressed in such warm and encouraging terms in his second letter. Whilst many have linked some of these together, clearly the first two cannot be the same man, but *ours* could be any one (or more?) of the other three. However, we cannot have certainty about any of this and therefore it is wiser to keep them apart. What we do know, is that Gaius here in Romans 16:23 had opened his home to both Paul and the whole church at Corinth; whilst we may be sure that the church and Paul did 'enjoy' (NIV) the hospitality of the Gaius home, that is not quite what Paul said: he merely commented 'Gaius, my host and of the whole church.' We thought of the value of an open home when considering Aquila and Priscilla in the previous chapter.

Intriguingly, a first century paving block has been discovered at Corinth with the inscription 'Erastus laid this pavement at his own expense', and he is called an *aedile* which is a commissioner of public works. However, here in Romans 16:23 the word used is *oikonomos*, which is more akin to a treasurer—but the two posts do not need to be exclusive of each other. It is encouraging that **Erastus** (v 23) had been converted, since as a government official in Corinth he held a significant post. Later, Paul would refer to an Erastus 'who remained at Corinth' (2 Timothy 4:20; see also Acts 19:22)—had his duties held him back? Of **Quartus** (v 23) we know nothing more than that he was in the queue eager to send his greetings to Rome.

Finally

These thirty-four little Christians whose names appear in Romans 16, certainly needed Paul's final encouragement: 'Now to him who is able to establish you by my gospel and the proclamation of Jesus Christ … to the only wise God be glory for ever through Jesus Christ! Amen.' (vs 25–26). The days of bitter persecution would soon be on them. How many of these names would shortly be inscribed on the roll of honour of those 'who have come out of the great tribulation; [and] have washed their robes and made them white in the blood of the Lamb' (Revelation 7:14) we cannot know. But we do know that very soon, far from the gentle words of encouragement from Paul, many of these little people would hear the roar of the immense crowds chanting for their blood as the wild animals were turned loose on them to soak the blood of the martyrs into the dry sand of the Roman amphitheatre. But they had served their Master well, and God's little people were neither overlooked here—nor at the gates of glory.

Unknown warriors— mentioned in dispatches

'We are sending along with [Titus] the brother who is praised by all the churches for his service to the gospel. What is more, he was chosen by the churches to accompany us as we carry the offering, which we administer in order to honour the Lord himself and to show our eagerness to help. ... In addition, we are sending with them our brother who has often proved to us in many ways that he is zealous, and now even more so because of his great confidence in you' 2 Corinthians 8:16–22.

F ive metres inside the main entrance of Westminster Abbey in London and set into the floor, is a large block of black marble. Cut into the marble and picked out in gold leaf are these words:

'Beneath this stone lies the body of a British Warrior unknown by name or rank. Brought from France to lie among the most illustrious of the land and buried here on Armistice day 11th November 1920 in the presence of his majesty King George IV, his ministers of State, the chiefs of his forces and a vast concourse of the nation. Thus are commemorated the many multitudes who during the Great War of 1914–1918 gave the most that man can give, life itself for God, for King and country, for loved ones, home and empire, for the sacred cause of justice and the freedom of the world.'

That is the grave of what has become known as the Unknown Warrior. Other countries have similar graves, but that one is the tribute of Great Britain. The unknown warrior represents those who lived, fought and died for the cause of justice and freedom and whose names were entirely lost to history. Thousands died and their torn bodies were never discovered, or having been recovered, no-one ever knew who they were—all means of identification had been lost in the carnage of a brutal battlefield. They received no battle honours, and there are no records of them in military history; we only know that they fought and they died—and we know why they fought and died.

But our Unknown Warrior was not always unknown. Somewhere, sometime he had a mother, who carried him, nursed him, cared for him. He had a father who played with him and loved him. Perhaps he had doting grandparents. Possibly he made a great impression in his village or town for his trade or profession, or his ability at sport, or just because he was a nice guy to have around. Then, he went off to war with the love and tears of his family. But soon no one knew him; he was nothing more than an unnamed broken body on a battlefield. Then he came back to England as the Unknown Warrior. His name is lost to history, but the cause he fought for and the contribution he made lives on through those words engraved on a black marble slab in a building whose first foundations were consecrated the year before the Battle of Hastings. He lies, unknown and unnamed among some of the most illustrious names of British history.

Known, yet unknown

In 2 Corinthians 8, we have two men whose names are not recorded. We do not know where they came from, we do not know who they were, we do not know how or where they died, and apart from three verses in Scripture we know absolutely nothing about them. They are the Unknown Warriors of the New Testament. But like that soldier in Westminster Abbey, they represent the multitudes who for the cause of the gospel and the Lord Jesus Christ have lived and fought and died well. It is to Christians like these— millions across the expanse of the globe and the span of the millennia— young and old, men and women, rich and poor, educated and uneducated, that we owe the expansion of the true church of Jesus Christ and our own hearing of the message of salvation. Countless thousands of people since the first century have passed on the message of the good news of Jesus Christ until one day somebody told us. And no one knows who they all were. For us, they have been lost in the mists of history, but their names are well recorded in the database of heaven . These are the indispensable little people of the gospel.

Inevitably, there is no lack of suggestions among the commentators as to the identity of these two men: Mark, Luke, Epenetus, Trophimus, Apollos, Silas have all been suggested, and the great Reformer John Calvin is absolutely certain that one is Barnabas. However, if God had wanted us to know their names, he would certainly have told us. Although I cannot tell you their names, I can tell you the kind of men they were.

At the time Paul was writing his second letter to the church at Corinth, somewhere around the year AD 58, he had had a very uneasy relationship with the church in that city: they had rejected his advice, questioned his authority, and ridiculed his preaching The apostle had written a pretty firm letter to them, which had initially achieved the very opposite of his intentions, then he paid them a visit—which was even more painful for him to recall; he wrote a second letter which we do not have, and now he writes yet again. That second letter he described in 2 Corinthians 2:4, 'I wrote to you out of great distress and anguish of heart and with many tears, not to grieve you but to let you know the depth of my love for you.' The more they hurt him, the more Paul loved them, the more they rejected him the more he cared for them, and the more they told him to stop pulling apostolic rank and to leave them alone, the more he pleaded with them to listen to him. This, then, is Paul's third letter to the Corinthians. He had been waiting in Berea for a reply and finally Titus came with the good news that the Corinthian church has seen their error, were desperately sorry for their slack behaviour that brought discredit to the gospel and they had started to put things right. Paul was overjoyed.

Titus was going to take this letter back to the Corinthians—and he would be accompanied by two other brethren who at the time were clearly well known. Of the first of these Unknown Warriors we are just told two things. First, he had a wide reputation for gospel work (2 Corinthians 8:18). He was praised by all the churches for his service to the gospel. Literally Paul wrote, 'the brother whose praise (or commendation) is in the gospel throughout (or among) all the churches.' In other words, throughout all the churches they were talking about this brother and they were commending him to one another for his gospel work. You might think it is all the more odd that we do not know his name if all the churches were talking about him. That, of course is the point from Paul's perspective. They would all know who it was simply by reputation, and when he arrived, the Christians at Corinth would all say, 'Oh we guessed he was the one Paul would send.'

But why did God not direct Paul to give *us* his name? Because this man's name is legion. He represents a great multitude who are well known in their time and to their church; they are loved and respected by the people they work among for their hard work in the gospel, but their name and rank is lost entirely to history. And God has deliberately planted these two men in 2 Corinthians 8 to make that very point. It would have been so easy for the Spirit to have prompted the apostle Paul to slip the names in as he was writing this letter—but he did not. God is teaching us that it mattered that it did not matter who they were.

The motivation of so many is the hope of reputation: stardom or success; a name in the news or business, in politics or academics, in sport or education, in literature or art—even in religion. They long to leave their name for generations to admire. But what does it matter to have a name imprinted in history? In the grand scheme, few are famous for more than five minutes. To day-dream of fame is a trivial pursuit.

Here are two men, and we do not know their names or what they achieved. We do not know where they came from, where they lived, or what later happened to them. They simply flit across the stage of Scripture and pass on into the mists of history. But they had a good reputation among those who knew them in their day. And they had a good reputation not for the number of their academic qualifications or the companies they chaired, not for the articles they wrote in their professional journal, or for the headlines they made in the national press, not even for the team they played for or what they achieved in the Olympic Games in Athens, but because they worked hard in the gospel. And whenever Christians talked about them they thought of the gospel.

Paul lost 'everything' to gain Christ; he tells us so in Philippians 3. Everything, meant reputation, education, security, even his religion. He counted it as trash to get Christ and to know him. Our unknown warrior was praised for his service to the gospel. Every time people talked about him, whenever his name came up in conversation, they said, 'Oh yes, a good gospel man he is'. He was not known for his sharp edges and abrasive character; he was not discussed for his selfish nature, stubborn will, cold heart or rebellious spirit. He did not even have the tributes of the world flowing in on him. He was known only because of his gospel work and the Saviour for whom he was working. And two thousand years later we still know him for that—even though we do not know his name. Nothing matters more than that we should pass out of this life known as one who worked hard for the gospel—even though our name will soon be forgotten.

Whenever I find myself in a graveyard, whether ancient or modern, I always have the same thought. I look at the rows of graves and read some of the inscriptions. But in a really old cemetery the inscriptions are mostly worn away by the years, sometimes centuries, of wind and rain; lichen has added its growth to obliterate the loving words carved by grieving family and friends. I wonder who they were and what they meant in life. Today, no one knows them; their mourners have themselves been mourned long ago. But I wonder what legacy they left behind? Is this world a little better because they lived here? And more important: where have they gone?

An old man resting in a cemetery read these words on one gravestone:

'Remember friend, when passing by
As you are now, so once was I.
As I am now, you soon will be,
Prepare for death and follow me.'
The old man was sufficiently wise to add the following two lines:
'To follow you, I'm not content,
Until I know which way you went.'

The second thing we learn about this unknown warrior is that he had a wide reputation for total honesty. Verse 19 reads, 'What is more, he was chosen by the churches to accompany us as we carry the offering, which we administer in order to honour the Lord himself and to show our eagerness to help.' During his travels, Paul had been collecting money from the Asian churches to carry a love-gift for the Christians in Judea who were facing extreme poverty and hardship. And being a wise man, Paul wanted to ensure that he could never be charged with lining his own pocket; for Paul, the books must be properly audited: 'We want to avoid any criticism of the way we administer this liberal gift. For we are taking pains to do what is right, not only in the eyes of the Lord but also in the eyes of men' (vs 20–21). It should never be left to the Charity Commissioners or the VAT inspectors to tell churches how they should keep their accounts open for scrutiny.

When Paul was administering this gift, and money was being given to him for the churches in Judea, he was well aware that somebody somewhere would accuse him of dishonesty and embezzlement. As it happens the Corinthians were the first to make that suggestion. So Paul decided he would make sure that wherever he went he had trustworthy men, men of impeccable honesty who the churches had chosen, so that in the eyes of the Lord and in the eyes of the world no one could point a finger. It is never enough for the Christian to say, 'My conscience is clear on this'. The question is: 'Can the world *see* that your conscience is clear?'

Paul looked for a man of total, absolute and proven integrity; a man of whom you would say, 'I would trust him with my last denarius and leave him with the key to my home', of whom you knew his word was his bond and his mind, his attitude and his whole being was utterly trustworthy. And Paul found such a man in our unknown warrior. But in verse 19 Paul tells us that he was chosen by the church; the word means that he was elected by a vote. We do not know how they did it, but here is the value of elections. Every leader in the church should know that they have the support of those they lead. That is true in the world, and it should be so in the church. There was no question who they would choose. *We* do not know his name, but *they* did. And when they looked for a man of that kind of impeccable honesty, he was top of the list.

Everybody knew him because everybody could trust him. He was a man without stain, or a hint of dishonesty, whose word was his bond and whose name was a guarantee of trust. A lot of cash was involved: Paul says it was 'a liberal gift'. The bigger the sum the more careful you have to be. How many Christians have unregistered software on their computer, illegal videos in their rack, outstanding bills in their files, untaxed or uninsured vehicles, or unlicensed television sets? Is that doing what is right in the eyes of the Lord and men?

When God has an army of Christian warriors like this unknown warrior, the nation will learn what Christianity is all about, even if none of those soldiers goes down in the records of history. Each is known in heaven by the Lord who died on the cross for them and they will have made a significant mark on this earth.

The contagion of enthusiasm

We know even less about the second of our two Unknown Warriors: 'In addition, we are sending with them our brother who has often proved to us in many ways that he is zealous, and now even more so because of his great confidence in you'(v 22). This man was enthusiastically active. And enthusiasm, like grumbling, is contagious. An enthusiast is someone who takes great joy in what they are doing and puts their heart and soul into it. Have you ever taken a child out for the day and everything you show them is boring?

The Battle of Bosworth took place in August 1485, but I stood on what some consider to be that battle field and watched a re-enactment of the encounter that ended the Wars of the Roses and put Henry Tudor of the House of Lancaster on the throne of England. As I watched the mock battle, behind me a despairing grandmother tried to gain the interest of a little boy in the fine horses and their knights, the pikemen and swordsmen clashing against each other, the archers firing volleys into the air and the guns roaring; but her grandson was bored and wanted to go! Clearly she was at a loss to know where she could take him that would cap this show for interest. All her enthusiasm had failed in the face of his withering boredom. That was a bad day for grandmother. What a difference when you take a youngster somewhere, anywhere, and they are wide-eyed with wonder at just everything they see. Their excitement rubs off on you and you find a new interest in the childish things that would otherwise be adult-boring. Move them onto something else and they are just as excited and enthusiastic about that. At the end of the day you are worn out, but you have had a great day. Zeal and enthusiasm are great gifts to the church.

Jesus was a great enthusiast. It was written of him that 'Zeal for your house consumes me' (John 2:17). The whole life of our Lord was enthusiastically dedicated to the one great purpose of building a church of living disciples for the glory of his Father. Actually the word used by Paul here in 2 Corinthians 8:22 is not the normal word for zeal (*zelos*) but is *spoudaios* which refers to speed or haste in doing something; but it came to mean much the same thing. Whoever is quick to get on with something is clearly a zealous person.

When you work with an enthusiast you catch some of the fire from them. A colleague of mine, who had no interest in organs or love for organ music, found himself in an exhibition of old organs; organs of every shape and date were there, and the man speaking about them was such an enthusiast for his cause that my friend was riveted by the man's zeal—so much so that at the end he had to take a firm hold on himself not to buy a cassette recording! The church would be a miserable place without people like our unknown warrior of consistent enthusiasm.

Notice that the apostle said that he had: 'often proved to us in many ways' his enthusiasm—'and now even more so'. Paul was piling on the accolades. 'Often' would be enough, but 'in many ways' adds to it, and 'now even more so' is in danger of being excessive. Here was a man who was not only enthusiastic about his own programme—we can all get enthusiastic about *our* programmes. But he was enthusiastic about the programmes of others. We can be very enthusiastic about the department of the church we work in, but can we be enthusiastic about the department somebody else is working in? We can all be very enthusiastic for our own successes, but can we be enthusiastic for someone else's success? Are we equally enthusiastic for the work of the gospel wherever we see it going forward even if it is not in our patch, through our hands, out of our stable?

Here was a man whose enthusiasm was contagious and I believe that was one of the reasons he was sent with Titus. This man, whoever he was, was an encourager because he was a zealous enthusiast. I have no doubt that the church at Corinth thought, 'Oh I am glad he's coming with Titus.' Do you know people like that? You love them in your home or church because they are such a breath of fresh air, such an encouragement; so zealous for God. He is an unknown warrior today, but he did untold good in the first century church. The church needs an army of Christians who love working for Christ and for whom hardships and challenges and disappointments are incentives.

In December 1854 Captain Hedley Vicars of the 97th Infantry Regiment was surviving in the cold mud-filled trenches outside Sebastopol in the hourly danger of the Crimean War. The British army was waiting around the walls of the city and men were dying daily from disease and enemy fire. It was one of those disastrous wars of English history because those in charge could not make up their minds what to do whilst the men in the trenches knew exactly what to do. On December 2nd Hedley Vicars, a deeply committed and very enthusiastic Christian after his amazing conversion, wrote a letter home to his family. Before the days of censorship from the front line he commented on the non-progress of the campaign: 'It's no use doing things by halves, you have got to go at it hammer and tongs'. And then he added: 'The men of all the British Regiments are dying in numbers every day and many are buried without a funeral service. We are now, to mend matters, placed on half rations. But I was never much of an epicure so I am quite contented with what they give me, indeed I have no patience with fellows who are always grumbling. Our hardships are certainly very great, but as soldiers we ought to bear them without a murmur. Many officers I hear are now resigning their commissions, I can only say shame on those who desert their country in the time of need.'

Every letter that officer wrote was an incredible revelation of the fervour of a man who was an enthusiastic soldier. But he was also enthusiastically in love with his Saviour—even in the mud of Crimea. The only thing he complained about was those who were grumbling! When Hedley Vicars received his commission, men from all over England volunteered to join his regiment because they wanted to serve under him. Our unknown warrior in Paul's letter was serving a better cause and for a greater king, and he offered an undefeated zeal and enthusiasm for gospel work. That is a great gift from God.

'Men like this' wrote Paul in v 23, 'are representatives of the church and an honour to Christ.' Men and women of the kind of hard, diligent work and total integrity and enthusiasm displayed here will always honour Christ—they cannot help it. Thank God for the millions of unknown warriors who have represented Christianity and honoured Christ so well. Christians yesterday and today all over the world have been, and are, tortured and martyred for their faith in Christ, yet still they go on telling the good news. Faithful men carried the Bible across our nation in the time of

John Wycliffe in the fourteenth century and died for it—we know few of their names, but God knows them all. A little boy of nine years was burnt at the stake in 1526 for reading the Lord's prayer in English; we do not know his name, but God does. And today from Burma to Bangladesh, from India to Indonesia, from Cuba to Korea, from Saudi Arabia to the Sudan, Christians die in squalor and obscurity because they will not deny their Lord. But these unknown warriors are all known to God and heaven is waiting to welcome them home.

Unknown, yet well known

Those words on the tomb of the Unknown Warrior in Westminster Abbey: 'Unknown by name or rank, brought from France to lie among the most illustrious of the land in the presence of his majesty King George IV, his ministers of State, the chiefs of his forces and a vast concourse of the nation', are the honours of a realm for an unknown warrior in the battles of this world. Better by a thousand times are the words addressed to the Christian warriors in Hebrews: 'But you have come to Mount Zion, to the heavenly Jerusalem, the city of the living God. You have come to thousands upon thousands of angels in joyful assembly, to the church of the firstborn, whose names are written in heaven. You have come to God, the judge of all men, to the spirits of righteous men made perfect, to Jesus the mediator of a new covenant, and to the sprinkled blood' (Hebrews 12:22).

In a short series of television programmes portraying the experiences of a war-time cameraman, the narrator reminisced on the terrible scenes he witnessed at the ill-fated landings at Anzio in Italy in 1944; he commented on the sense of unity and the expressions of bravery shown by so many in those terrible weeks of incessant bombardment by the German artillery and aircraft and then he added: 'In wartime, brilliant fragments of courage pass by unnoticed.' That is so true of the history of the Christian church. For every courageous soldier of yesterday and today whose name has come down to us for bravery in the face of torture, the burning stake, the wild beast in the arena, cruel mockery in a filthy prison or the loss of loved ones and honour, there are literally thousands who are wholly unknown to us: Their 'brilliant fragments of courage have passed by unnoticed' by the gaze of the world and even the church; but the eyes of the Lord have not overlooked every daring act or steady resolve of spiritual nerve. Paul was not one to overlook the courage of a little man.

On that marble slab commemorating the Unknown Warrior the words from 2 Chronicles 24:16 are inscribed: 'And they buried him among the kings, because he had done good both toward God and toward his house.' That text referred to Jehoiadah originally, but they are more than appropriate for our Christian unknown warriors. Around the four sides of that marble slab are four more passages from the Bible. On one side are the words: 'Greater love hath no man than this, that a man lay down his life for his friends'; on another: 'In Christ shall all be made alive'; on another: 'Unknown and yet well known. Dying and behold we live'; and on another: 'The Lord knoweth them that are his'.

Unknown yet well known because the Lord knows those who are his. Heaven knows them, God knows them, the angels know them, the great company of the redeemed in eternity knows them—and the Master praises them. So, what do the praises of men matter?

Index